P9-DEY-541

Lively

Object Lessons

WESLEY T. RUNK

BAKER BOOK HOUSE
GRAND RAPIDS, MICHIGAN

2 44

Run

Copyright 1974 by
C.S.S. Publishing Company
Reprinted 1979 by
Baker Book House
with permission of copyright owner

ISBN: 0-8010-7672-2

Formerly published under the title,
Praise God Loudly

Printed in the United States of America

CONTENTS

HERE COMES JESUS

John 1:14-18, vs. 15b: He who comes after me ranks before me because he existed before me.

Object Fanfare and banners.

Good morning, boys and girls. How are you on this first beautiful Sunday in the New Year? Isn't it wonderful to get started off in the right way by coming to worship? I think it is so right that I want to show you how we ought to do it. [*If someone can play the trumpet, have him play some opening bars of a stirring fanfare. Perhaps the organist could use the trumpet stop on the organ. Then let someone come in carrying some banners. Example: Blessed New Year -- God Bless Us in 1975.*] How about that, boys and girls? Isn't it wonderful the way we get so excited about the first day in the new year or the first Sunday? These are really special times for all of us, aren't they? And yet the first day or first Sunday is special not so much because of itself but because of the many good days and Sundays that are yet to come.

There was a man called John the Baptist who was a lot like our trumpet sound or our banners. He is a very famous person in the Bible and in our Christian life because he told us of one who was to come. Do you know who John the Baptist talked about? [*Let them answer.*] That's right, Jesus. John the Baptist was the announcer, the man who told us about who was to come and why he was coming.

Now, I don't suppose many of you play a trumpet. How many play the trumpet? See, not very many. And I don't think that many of you want to walk around carrying a banner wherever you go, do you? Of course not. But all of you can be like John the Baptist, at least when it comes to telling people about Jesus.

Blowing trumpets and carrying banners gets the people's attention but that's all. But when you tell people about how much God loves you and about all the good things he does for you, then you will help others to know about Jesus just as you do.

As a matter of fact, you can be better than a trumpet or even a banner. They just make some noise or fly on by, but your voice and your love will make people want to wait for Jesus to come into their lives. So, remember John the Baptist and try to help people get ready for Jesus.

OUR BEST EXAMPLE

Luke 2:41-52, vs. 52: And Jesus increased in wisdom and stature and in favor with God and man.

Object: A box of "Wheaties," a loaf of Wonder Bread, a Bible, a philosophy book.

Good morning, boys and girls. I want to begin today by looking for some pretty special volunteers. They must be tall and strong. How many tall and strong people do we have? [*Pick several from the group.*] That's fine. I brought along a box of Wheaties and some Wonder Bread that builds bodies twelve ways in case any of you think that you may need something to be extra strong for our experiment today. Why don't you hold these groceries in case any of you think that you may need them. [*Have one of the children hold these items so that they are prominently displayed.*]

Now let's see what else our volunteers must be like. They must be very wise. They must not only be able to learn from books, but they must also remember what they learn and use it to help others. How many of these volunteers would you think are wise? [*Get some of the group reaction.*] That's very interesting. Not everybody thinks that we have the wisest people for volunteers. Well, just in case, let me give you an old philosophy book with the thoughts of the wisest men in the world written in it.

Now let's see what else our volunteers must be like. I know, they must be liked by others. How do we know when others like us? What is something that we can do to help other people to like us? [*Wait for some answer.*] It's a smile! Do all of our volunteers have a nice smile? Do people smile when they meet our volunteers? Let's have this volunteer put on a nice smile.

Well, that's fine. That's the way we like our volunteers: strong, wise and friendly. Oh, wait a minute.

There is one other thing. We need to know that God likes us, too. One of our volunteers must be able to show that God is in contact with him. Maybe if one of our volunteers were to show us how he talks things over with God we would know that God talks to him. How do we talk to God? Prayer, that's right. [*Select one child to take up prayer pose.*] Well, that's it. The perfect volunteer would be strong, wise, have other people like him and be trusted by God. Do you know anyone who is that perfect, who has all those things?

Did you know that there was once a boy just a few years older than you who was like the volunteer we all want to be? His name was Jesus. When he was 12 years old the Bible says that Jesus "increased in *wisdom and stature and in favor with God and man.*" Even when Jesus was a boy the world knew him to be all of these things. That's something to think about, isn't it? No wonder people thought Jesus was something special even when he was only 12 years old. He is really someone special to follow as an example.

DOING GOD'S WORK

John 2:1-11, vss. 7-8: Jesus said to them, "Fill the jars with water" and they filled them up to the brim. He said to them, "Now draw some out, and take it to the steward of the feast." So they took it.

Object: A drawing of Jesus without hands, feet, eyes, ears, nose and mouth. [Trace over a large copy and simply leave these parts off the drawing.]

Good morning, artists! Every day is a beautiful day for an artist, isn't it? He can see all the beautiful colors in God's great plan and on God's good earth. This morning I am going to tell you a story, an old story, that has been told many times before. But it is one which you will enjoy hearing again.

The story is about an artist who was asked to make a special painting of Jesus for a brand new church. This painting was supposed to be put on the wall of the nave. When the artist began his work he asked everyone to leave and went right to work. After several weeks he told the Pastor that he was finished and invited the congregation to come and look at what he had done. The people came and when they saw what he had done, they gasped with great surprise. [*Take out the drawing of Jesus without the features.*] "Why, you haven't finished the painting! You have only begun."

"No," the artist said, "I am finished." There on the wall, high and lifted up, was Jesus. The robes Jesus wore were beautiful, he was tall and strong looking. But something was missing. The people saw a person without hands or feet, eyes or nose, mouth or ears.

Again they said, "You haven't finished the painting because Jesus doesn't have eyes or a nose or hands or feet or mouth or ears."

"That's right," the painter said. "You must do those things for Jesus. You are the hands and feet and the eyes and ears of Jesus."

Some people think this is a brand new idea that only began after Jesus went back to heaven to live with his heavenly Father. But that's not true. Jesus has always asked people to help him do his work. Today we learn that he asked people at a wedding feast to help him turn water into wine. Another time he asked a boy to give him his lunch and he fed 5,000 people with it. Jesus has always asked boys and girls and moms and dads to help, and today it is the same as it always has been.

We listen with our ears and run with our feet to deliver his message with our mouths. We see with our eyes what work he wants done, and then do it with our hands. That's why the artist's painting of Jesus was so good, because it reminded people that Jesus wants us to help him do God's work.

THE LAST WILL BE FIRST

Matthew 20:1-16, vs. 16: So the last will be first, and the first last.

Object: Record player; records that children would like and some they wouldn't like.

Today, boys and girls, is one month since Christmas day. The time surely flies fast, doesn't it? It seems like only yesterday that we sang Christmas carols, opened gifts, and came to worship the Christ Child at Christmas services, doesn't it? I brought some Christmas gifts with me to help you learn one of the great Christian truths as taught by Jesus a long time ago which is still very important today.

I brought with me a record player and a lot of "45" records. Now I am going to let you choose which records you would like to hear. Which one shall we choose first? [*Read the names of the records and as they choose the ones they like put them on top. Emphasize what you are doing so they know that the bottom records are the records they like least.*]

Good, now we have all your favorite records on the top and the ones you don't like so well on the bottom. But now watch what happens when I pick up these records and put them on the record player. [*Put the records on carefully so that the children see what is happening.*] See, the ones you chose last will now be the first ones played and the first ones will be the last ones played.

Jesus saw that some men and women thought that because they worked hard or had a lot of money or a fine name and men honored them that God should also choose them first. God asked the Jews to be messengers of his word first, but he also made his message available to all the other people in the world later. Now God says he is going to begin with the last people who heard his message. Those last people, according to our understanding, are the Christians. Just as the records that you didn't like so much when you had your choice would be the first played, so will the Christians be the first called by God to receive his gift of eternal life.

I hope you understand that it is God's gift and he not only chooses who he will give it to, but how many he wants to give it to. All of the records were made to be played. While we may like one better than another, they will all be played by the one who runs the record player. I hope you understand that the most important part is that God wants to give his love to as many people who accept him. It doesn't matter who they are as long as they let him love them.

GOD'S WORD IS A SEED

Luke 8:4-15, vs. 11b: The seed is the word of God.

Object: Rocks, weeds, hard chunks of dirt and some good soil.

Good morning, boys and girls. Today the children's sermon will be in the form of a little play. That's right, I am going to tell the story and you are going to be the actors. Let me show you what I mean. God says that when he speaks, his word is like a seed. That's right, a seed. Have you ever thought of God being like a farmer? Well, that is what he says he is like. Now if God is the farmer, then what are we? Well, in the story that Jesus told about God as a farmer, he said that we are like the different kinds of soil.

Now comes your part in the play. I want some of you to be different kinds of soil and we will see what kind of seed will grow in you. The first kind of soil is like this. [*Hold up the big chunks of hard ground.*] It is hard and full of clay. Have you ever known any boys and girls who heard about Jesus but just paid no attention at all and went right on doing what they were doing as if the name of Jesus had never been mentioned? They think they are hard and tough and they want other people to think the same thing about them. I need some boys and girls to act like that kind of dirt. Will you stand over here and look very tough and hard? That's fine. [*Give them the chunks.*]

Now there is another kind of dirt that we have on a farm. It looks like dirt on the top, but right under what you see there is rock. This kind of dirt is like the boys and girls who are always ready to do something. They start out real well and then in a moment they lose interest in what they are doing. They are the kind who love to come to church on Sunday, and when they are in God's house they look like the best Christians in the world. But when they leave they forget everything that God told them. Will some of you pretend like you are very rocky soil? That's fine. Let's see how a rock looks. Good. [*Hand them the rocks.*]

Now I need another kind of soil and this is the kind we not only find on the farm but sometimes it even happens in my front yard. This soil has lots of weeds. These are the kinds of boys and girls who let the farmer or God plant his seed but then they go places and do things that they should never do. It is this kind of soil that very often says bad words and tells lies. Now I need some very weedy soil. Can you look weedy? Good. [*Give them the weeds.*]

Now I need one more kind of soil and, of course, that means that I will need one more group of volunteers. This soil is smooth and rich. It is like the group of boys and girls who listen to what God has to say and obey it as soon as they hear it. They not only come to church on Sunday, but they also use the lessons they learn there during the week. Now, can I have the good earth stand over here in a group? They can hold in their hands the good earth.

Now the big question is, where do you think the seed that God the farmer is going to send is going to grow and produce good fruit? Will God's seed grow in the tough old hard soil? [*Hold the Bible over the groups' heads as each succeeding group is mentioned.*] Will it grow in the rocky soil? Will it grow in the weedy soil? Will it grow in the good earth? So, just as it grows in the good earth, then it also grows best in boys and girls. Make sure that your life is like the good soil, and stay away from being the hard, the rocky and the weedy.

A GAME FOR FOLLOWERS

Luke 18:31-43, vs. 43: And immediately he received his sight and followed him, glorifying God; and all the people, when they saw it, gave praise to God.

Object: A game of "Simon Says."

Good morning, boys and girls. Isn't this a beautiful way to begin the week? How many of you have been making valentines for the other boys and girls in your class at school? It will be a lot of fun when you get to see all the nice ones that others have been making for you.

Say, when you have parties at school or at a friend's house, do you ever play games? You do? I wonder if you have ever played one of my favorite games, "Simon says." Now here are the directions: you must do everything that I do as long as I say "Simon says"; but if I don't say "Simon says" and still do something, then you must not do it. If you do it, then you have made a mistake and you must drop out of the game. I am going to be the leader and you must be the followers. Simon says, touch your nose; Simon says, touch your toes; Simon says, touch your ears; touch your mouth. Oh, did I catch anyone? Did anyone make a mistake and touch his mouth without Simon saying to do it? Well, let's try once more. [*Repeat the same process a few times until you catch a couple more children. Don't leave it with only one or two being caught.*]

Listening to directions is very important if we are to be good followers. Did you know that it is just as important to be a good follower as it is to be a leader? A long time ago Jesus had twelve very important followers who we remember by name almost two thousand years later. Today we read about a man who was healed by Jesus after being blind for a long time. This poor man had nothing to do in those days except be a beggar. He cried out and asked Jesus to help him and Jesus did. Do you know what the beggar did then? He jumped up and thanked God and began to follow Jesus wherever he went. And when the people who were standing around saw how excited he was and how happy he was over being given his sight and becoming a follower of Jesus, they also began to sing and praise God. Because the one blind beggar was a happy follower of Jesus, he helped many other people to be happy followers of Jesus, too.

Now we can be good followers of Jesus and help other people become happy in the Lord also if we are sure in following Jesus. We must be ready to praise God at all times and sing his praises to the whole world. We must be ready to forgive and to love all of God's people. And do you want to know the wonderful thing about being a follower of Jesus? You can make a mistake and he doesn't make you leave his band of followers. No, not Jesus! He forgives your mistakes and invites you to keep right on trying to play the game right. That's the kind of a game that I like, because that's the kind of a follower I am. I make mistakes, but Jesus always forgives them and forgets them.

TAKING RISKS

Matthew 4:1-11, vs. 7: Jesus said to him, "Again it is written, 'You shall not tempt the Lord your God.' "

Object: A quarantine sign and/or a highway sign such as "Reduce Speed."

Good morning to you, boys and girls. Sunday really is a beautiful day no matter what the weather is outside. Even when it is cold, the church is warm, not just because the furnace is on but because you are so welcome and everybody wants you to be here. It takes a long time to get acquainted in some places but not in the church. Here everybody is your friend and you are a friend to everybody. That is the way Jesus teaches us to be. He tells us that Christians are meant to love everyone. St. Paul says that we must always be ready to help people, especially those in our congregation of faith.

I brought some signs with me this morning that will help you to better understand what Jesus wants us to know. For instance, there is this quarantine sign that says *STAY OUT -- HIGHLY CONTAGIOUS DISEASE.* You know what that means, don't you? That means if you go into the room where someone is sick with the mumps you will probably get the same disease in a short time. Have you ever noticed when you get a cold or the measles how soon your brother or sister gets the same disease? When the disease is serious a sign is put up on your door so others know that if they are smart, they will stay out.

Let me show you another sign. It says *DANGEROUS CURVE AHEAD -- REDUCE SPEED.* Now let's say that the regular speed limit is 55 miles an hour and you are driving at the speed when you see this sign. Should you step on the gas and go 65 miles an hour so that you can get around the curve faster, or should you slow down to maybe 40 miles an hour? That's right, you should slow down. If you went faster you might make it around the curve, but the chances are that you would crash.

A lot of people listen to what God has to say and they know that he means it for their own good. But they think maybe *just this one more time* they could get away with it. Jesus calls this tempting God. When we walk into a room where there is a contagious disease or drive at an unsafe speed, we are playing dangerously with our own lives. We may get so sick or have such a bad accident that we foolishly give up our lives that God gave us.

Well, the devil tried to tempt Jesus into forgetting God and following him. He made it sound pretty attractive. He also tried to get Jesus to jump off the highest building in town just to see if God really cared. Now, God would have had to forget all about gravity and the way he made the world to be able to save Jesus. That is what we call tempting God. Certain things are meant to happen because they make the world run right when they do. If God had wanted to do anything else he would have had to make things different for just that one time and Jesus knew that it was not right to tempt God.

It is really a good lesson for us to remember when we think of all the things that we want God to change just for us. Remember when you didn't want to go to school and you prayed for snow or the school bus to break down? Or do you remember when you forgot to make your bed so you hoped that your mother wouldn't go upstairs and check? These, according to Jesus, are the ways that we take risks that we shouldn't. Jesus was tempted, too, but he knew what God wanted for him.

PATIENCE AND PRACTICE

Matthew 15:21-28, vs. 28: Then Jesus answered her, "O woman, great is your faith! Be it done for you as you desire."

Object: An exercise requiring careful coordination; or learning to clap in rhythm -- any skill that requires patience and practice.

Good morning, boys and girls. February has been a very special month with many things happening. First of all, two of our greatest presidents were born in this month. Can you tell me who they were? [*Wait for answers.*] That's good, Washington and Lincoln. There was also a very special day for boys and girls on the 14th of the month that was an exciting time. That's right, Valentine's Day! There was another special day that came this month and we have been talking a lot about it recently. It was called Ash Wednesday, the beginning of Lent.

You have to be thinking all the time in February or something will pass you right up. When things come that fast you have to remember that you can never give up. I know a story about a lady and Jesus that is a good one to tell you today. It's about a lady who never gave up. This lady had a very sick daughter and she wanted Jesus to help her get better. But Jesus pretended that he could not help her. That's because he wanted to test her faith. She kept running after him and asking until Jesus finally healed her daughter. Sometimes things that we want a whole lot are hard to come by and we don't always get them the first time. Let me show you what I mean.

Do you think that you can do what I do the very first time you try? Here is a little game that I like to play. It takes a sharp mind and ears and fast hands to make it work. I am going to clap in a rhythm and then I want you to clap back at me the same thing that you heard me do.

We will do it several times. [*Start very simple with two claps and build to a complicated rhythm.*] Wow, you are pretty good! But it gets tougher as you go along, right? That is the way it is as you get older; things get more and more complicated and you have to try harder. Let's try another one that is my favorite. Some of you may have tried this before. First of all I want you to rub your tummy in a big circle. Then I want you to pat the top of your head with the other hand. Now let's try to do both of them at the same time. That's kind of hard, isn't it? It takes a lot of practice to be able to do that right.

Sometimes we find it hard to understand why God just doesn't answer our prayers right away. Maybe if he did they would not be so important to us and we would not appreciate them. But whatever the reason, we must learn not to give up. Very often it takes a lot of work and practice to make things work and to have God help us in the way that we want to be helped. We must learn to be like the lady in the story who wanted her little girl helped. She didn't give up but instead she kept after Jesus until he finally told her that because of her persistence he would help her. Remember that when you need something from God and you don't get it the first time you ask if it is for the best. God will give it to you at the right time if you keep on asking.

CHOOSING TO SERVE GOD

Luke 11:14-28, vs. 17: But he, knowing their thoughts, said to them, "Every kingdom divided against itself is laid waste, and house falls upon house."

Object: An old stool or some other object which you can saw in half and allow to stand simply by having the two sides lean against one another.

Good morning to you, boys and girls. Here we are in a new month, March. It used to seem funny to me that the year was all divided up into twelve different months with different names to go with each one. But it makes the year interesting and it is kind of nice all divided up. But let me tell you a story about a friend of mine who liked to divide things in a way that was not always very good. His name is Sam Stool. Now Sam is a kind of quiet guy who likes most people and most people like him. As a matter of fact, Sam liked people too much in a funny kind of way and it got him in trouble.

Let me tell you what happened. Sam had a boy friend named Mike and a girl friend named Sally and he liked them a lot. Sam really belonged to Mike, but Sally was so pretty and she was not quite as big as Mike and therefore when she sat on Sam there was not so much weight on his back. Both Mike and Sally always wanted to sit on Sam and they would argue and cry and shout and sometimes even push and shove over who would get to sit on Sam when they watched TV or sat by the fire and listened as their mom read a story. Well, one day Sam had an idea which he thought was a pretty good one. He had Sargent Saw come over and do a job. Well, you can imagine what happened the next .time Mike and Sally ran into the room to watch TV and they both made a dive for Sam Stool. You guessed it. [*Hit the stool or grab it and it will fall apart.*] Old Sam was done for, at least until the glue man came to fix Sam up. Here he tried to serve both sides, Sally and Mike, and instead he couldn't help anyone, for he had collapsed. Two sides when they are divided against themselves cannot stand, but instead they just collapse.

The reason that I tell you this story about my friend Sam Stool is that it helps me to tell you in another way something Jesus once said. People used to wonder if the things that Jesus did that were so wonderful and yet kind of frightening were because God gave him the power or because the devil gave him the power. Jesus said to the people, "The devil would want people to feel sick and he would want people to do bad, so why should he help me get rid of things that were bad? What I do is good and God is good, so it is God in heaven who helps me to do the things that I do."

Today we know that Jesus was sent from God and we know that he did the things he did because he loved us and wanted us to be happy and loved by others. But sometimes we have to ask ourselves whether we are doing the good things that our God wants us to do, or are we doing the bad things that the Devil wants us to do? We can't do both things, because if we do our lives will collapse just as my friend Sam Stool did. If we try to do something good because we know that Jesus would want us to do it, like helping or visiting a sick friend, and then we fight with the sick friend over a toy, then all of the good that we started to do gets lost in the bad. Jesus taught us that we cannot serve both God and the devil, because if we do we will get terribly mixed up and soon collapse. We can only serve God and really be happy. When we serve God we make other people happy as well.

BITS AND PIECES

John 6:1-15, vss. 12-13: And when they had eaten their fill, he told his disciples, "Gather up the fragments left over, that nothing may be lost." So they gathered them up and filled twelve baskets with fragments from the five barley loaves, left by those who had eaten.

Object: Umbrella, one shoe, one sock, one key, one hymnbook, one belt, one tie. You will need a man who will sit very inconspicuously in the congregation without these items until such time as the sermon for children reaches the point where he is called upon.

Good morning, boys and girls. I was walking around the church early this morning before anyone else was here, and I thought that I would pick up some things that people often leave. You can't imagine all the things that people forget and leave in the church. For instance, here is something that we find often. What do you call this? An umbrella. And then I found this shoe. Can you imagine leaving a shoe? [*Hand each item to one of the children to hold.*] In another room I found one sock, and in still another I found a key, and in the hall was this belt. In one of the Sunday School rooms I found a church hymnbook, and under the church pew I found this tie. What do you think of that? I probably could have found more if I had looked.

I guess they are not really much good since there is only one of each thing and we don't know who they belong to. What good is one shoe or one sock? That reminds me of a story about Jesus and his disciples. One day when they were out they walked a long way and the people followed them because they enjoyed being with Jesus and listening to what he had to teach and tell them. But Jesus knew that they had gone too far without having any food, so Jesus fed them all with one boy's lunch. He performed a miracle and thousands of people ate because this one small boy was willing to give his lunch to Jesus to be used to feed the people. Now after everyone had eaten, Jesus told the disciples to go out and collect what was left over, and there was still enough to fill twelve baskets.

No one except God knows how Jesus was able to feed all those people. But just think, there was still some left over and Jesus asked them to gather it up. Sometimes I think about those things that were left and I wonder why Jesus didn't just say throw the leftovers away. For instance, why don't we just throw the umbrella, shoe, sock, key, hymnbook, belt and tie away? Here I have walked around the church and picked them all up and now you are holding them and what good are they? Let's see if they are any good. [*Now address yourself to the congregation.*] Is there anyone here whom we could help if we keep these things that we are holding? [*Now is the time for "Mr. Untogether" to appear.*] Well, for heaven's sake, it is Mr. Untogether and he is missing a shoe. [*Mr. Untgether is put together by using each article with some explanation: the key is for his car, he had no hymnal where he was sitting to use, etc.*] This man is no longer a Mr. Untogether. Why, we will have to call him Mr. All Together.

Maybe it really is important when we gather up all of the little things like table prayers, going to Sunday School, singing a hymn of praise, forgiving our friends who hurt us and all the other little things that make loving Christians. Of course, the most important thing is to believe in Jesus as our Savior and to know that he loves us. But then the little pieces that are left around like our prayers and hymns help, too, to let others see what Christ has done for us.

A LESSON FROM JESUS

John 8:46-59, vs. 54: Jesus answered, "If I glorify myself, my glory is nothing; it is my Father who glorifies me, of whom you say that he is your God."

Object: A mirror.

Good morning to all of the boys and girls who think that I am good looking. How many of you think that I am the handsomest pastor in the whole world? How many of you think that I have the prettiest teeth and eyes that you have ever seen? Hmmm, it doesn't look like I am going to get to say good morning to many of you today. I don't understand why you don't think I am good looking. My mirror [*hold up the mirror*] thinks that I am very good looking. The other day I asked Minnie Mirror if she thought that I was the best looking pastor she had ever seen and she said "yes." Good old Minnie is quite a friend, isn't she? She thinks that I am pretty and tells me so whenever I ask her. But you know what? I don't believe her either. Mirrors are so funny, they can always tell you, if you let them, just what you want to hear. If you want them to tell you that you are tough you just make a tough face in a mirror and the mirror tells you that you are tough. If you make a sad face in a mirror then the mirror will tell you that you are sad, and if you make a happy face in the mirror then old Minnie will tell you that you are happy.

Do you know why mirrors are like that? It's because a mirror can only tell you what you tell it. It doesn't have a mind of its own or eyes of its own or a mouth of its own. Minnie just tells you what you tell it and no more. Some people like a mirror because of that reason and they fool themselves. They are afraid to ask a friend how they look because the friend might tell them that they have on too much lipstick or they frown too much or they forget to brush their teeth. But the mirror will only tell you what you want it to tell you.

People used to ask Jesus who he thought he was and he told them that he was whatever his Father in heaven wanted him to be. People used to get upset with him when he did that, but Jesus had a good reason. He knew that people would only believe what they wanted to believe about him, and that if he told them he was God some would be very happy and others would be very angry. Let me show you what I mean. Suppose a friend wants you to go somewhere and you know that you would have to ask your mother first and she probably would not let you go. The friend calls you a scaredy cat or tells you that you can go and come back before your mother will ever find out. You know what I mean? That person just wants you to go with him and he doesn't really care if you get hurt or if you disobey. He just wants you to be his mirror and do or say whatever he does.

Jesus knew that it was not really important how he felt or what other people felt who wanted Jesus to be a mirror. Jesus knew that the most important person was not another one like Minnie Mirror but God, our Father in heaven. Jesus was important and did important things because God the Father directed him and gave him the power to do it. A lot of us ought to learn a good lesson from Jesus and ask God what he thinks would be best and not from old Minnie Mirror. Having Minnie Mirror answer questions is like asking yourself and no one else. When you ask yourself you will only get the answer you want and not very often the one that is best for you. Jesus said that if you really want the right answer you will ask God and God will direct you.

THE GREAT PARADE

Matthew 21:1-9, vss. 8-9: Most of the crowd spread their garments on the road, and others cut branches from the trees and spread them on the road. And the crowds that went before him and that followed him shouted, "Hosanna to the Son of David! Blessed is he who comes in the name of the Lord! Hosanna in the highest!"

Object: Small bags of confetti [shredded newspaper in baggies will do].

Good morning to you, boys and girls. Isn't this an exciting day! Today is Palm Sunday. Whenever I think of Palm Sunday I think of how all the children in Jesus' time must have felt on the first Palm Sunday when Jesus and his disciples came to Jerusalem. What a day that must have been! You can almost close your eyes and imagine what happened. The people heard from others outside town that Jesus was coming. Jesus was the one who had healed the man of a broken hand and not too long ago he had actually brought a man back to life. Then there was the time he fed five thousand people with just a little boy's lunch. There were so many other things. He was loving and he cared for everybody who needed his help.

I wonder what it would be like if Jesus were coming to our town today. What would we do to make him feel welcome? Let's pretend that Jesus is coming to [*name of your town*] and we are going to welcome him. I have brought something for each of you, but you *must* keep it in the bag until you get outside. Here is some confetti. [*Rice would also work.*] We are going to pretend that we are sitting on the side of the road that Jesus is going to be walking down in a few minutes. Just imagine what it's going to be like. Won't it be great when he passes right by us? Just think, the same Jesus who told the story about the good Samaritan and how we are supposed to love our neighbor. And do you remember the time that the children kept shouting Jesus' name and the disciples tried to make the children quiet because they thought that he had more important things to do? Jesus told the disciples to let all the children come to him and some of them even sat on his lap.

The noise is getting louder and louder. Jesus must be coming! You can hear the people shouting, "Hosanna," and "Hooray for Jesus!" They are clapping and some of them are singing songs about making him a king. I will never forget the time when Jesus was teaching some people about how much God loved them when a Roman Captain of the Palace Guard came in all his splendor and asked Jesus to make a command that his sons would get well. What a powerful man he was with all those soldiers at his command. You wouldn't think that he would ever have to ask anybody for anything, but he asked Jesus and Jesus helped him.

Listen real closely and you can hear the crowds walking in the stone roads coming into town. It's almost like the sound of a waterfall hitting the river. Just think, pretty soon Jesus will be here and we will know that he doesn't want to be a king or earthly ruler. He wants to be the king of your heart and your mind. When he comes by let's shout "Hosanna to the Son of David! Blessed is he who comes in the name of the Lord!" [*Practice a few times.*]

Here he is, boys and girls! Let's let him know that we are here. "Hosanna to the Son of David! Blessed is he who comes in the name of the Lord!" [*Have them stand and show them to use their imaginations. By now I promise you that they will actually believe that they have been there and seen him.*]

THE BEST GIFT

Mark 16:1-7, vs. 6: And he said to them, "Do not be amazed; you seek Jesus of Nazareth, who was crucified. He has risen. He is not here; see the place where they laid him."

Object: A shoe box gift-wrapped but with the ribbon broken and the paper looking as if it had obviously been unwrapped.

Happy Easter, everyone! Isn't this a wonderful day? Certainly the most exciting day of the year! Easter was started on excitement and it has always remained the same. Can you imagine how excited the people were on the first Easter when they heard about Jesus' coming back to life? They could hardly believe it because no one had ever done it before. Can you imagine the excitement?

Speaking of excitement, I was sure excited this morning when I found this gift. How many of you like to find gifts, especially when they are intended for you? You can imagine my excitement when I found this in the study when I got to church this morning. It looks like a gift, but it seems that the ribbon is broken. Oh, well, that doesn't matter, does it? It's the gift inside that really counts. What do you think is in there? [*Let the children guess.*] I think it is a pair of shoes because it looks like a shoe box. Boy, could I use a nice new pair of shoes. I saw some the other day that were just beautiful. They were brassy brown with a big buckle and they shined like a pot of gold. Hmmm, it looks like the package has already been opened, doesn't it? The paper looks as if it had been crumpled and messed up. Oh, that really doesn't make any difference either. The real gift is inside the box. [*By now you have taken the paper off so all can see it is a shoe box.*] New shoes! I hope they are the kind I want with that big brass buckle. [*Open the box very slowly.*]

Oh, no! There isn't anything in the box! It's empty! I wonder what happened to the shoes? An empty shoe box. What a gift! [*With disappointment.*] Who ever would want an empty box of any kind?

Now, wait a minute. That's no way to think. I should be glad. When the shoes were in the box they were nothing. They were almost dead. But now the box is empty and that means that they are being used. Someone is getting to wear a new pair of shoes and I know the shoes are happy. An empty box makes a very happy story, because when the box is empty that means that whatever was in it is now up and doing what it is supposed to do.

You know, that is the way it was on the first Easter. The friends of Jesus went up to the place where Jesus was buried and when they got there they noticed that the big stone that had been put there was rolled away. The stone had been put there like the paper on our box. When they went inside, they didn't find Jesus and they were very sad. But then they were told that he was alive and gone and that what God had wanted to happen had happened. The tomb was empty, and Jesus was not dead but alive! So just as we are happy that the box was empty, we are much happier that the place where Jesus was buried is empty and he is alive. You see, the best gift that man ever got was something empty. That is hard to understand because we usually like things to be filled. But the best gift of all time was the empty grave of Christ. That means that Jesus is alive and that everyone who believes in him will never die but will always be made new.

SEEING THINGS CLEARLY

John 20:19-31, vs. 22: And when he had said this, he breathed on them and said to them, "Receive the Holy Spirit." :

Object: A pair of eyeglasses and a handkerchief.

Good morning, boys and girls. Do you remember the name we used for last Sunday? Easter! What a wonderful Sunday it was with so many people here that we hardly had room, and the people sang with such beautiful voices and flowers were everywhere. It really was a special day. Did you know that every Sunday should be Easter, or like a little Easter? That's right, the first Christians called every Sunday the Lord's Day because they remembered that it was on Sunday that they saw Jesus alive again after he had died on the cross and was put in the grave. The disciples used to worship every Friday night and Saturday, but after the Easter experience they started having their big service of worship on Sunday, the little Easter. We still do it today just as they started it almost 2,000 years ago.

Sometimes people find it hard to understand why we love Jesus so much. They read the Bible and some even go to church, but they still wonder why Jesus means so much to us. Some say they wish they could love God as much as we do, but for some reason they just don't know him the way they should. Well, we feel bad for those people, but we say there is something they can do about it if they want to. Let me show you a little experiment that might help you understand how God works with us. I have to use my special glasses that are kind of dusty and dirty. [*Have a volunteer examine the glasses and admit they they are hard to see through.*] Now you must remember that when the disciples first saw Jesus after the resurrection they didn't know what to believe. They were sad that Jesus had died, and since they didn't understand the wonderful way God can work, they were very puzzled to see Jesus alive again. But Jesus came and breathed on them and told them they were about to receive a special gift called the Holy Spirit. Once they had the Holy Spirit they would believe.

This is where the experiment comes in. Have you ever seen someone clean his glasses? How does he do it? That's right, he breathes hard on his glasses and when he wipes them off he has clean glasses. Though he couldn't see before, he can now see well. Just by breathing on the glasses and wiping them off, a person can see clearly whatever he wants to see. Now Jesus breathed on the disciples and when he did he breathed into them the Holy Spirit and they could not only see, they could see things they had never seen before.

The Holy Spirit is God's gift to people and it helps them to believe what they could not believe without him. We need the Holy Spirit if we're going to believe like the disciples. Without him we are like people who look through dirty glasses. They see a little, and if they don't take off their glasses and check they might even think they can see pretty well. But people with dirty glasses are missing so much in life that they could have if they just cleaned them by breathing on them and shining them with a handkerchief. It's the same way with God. Here God has this wonderful gift to give us called the Holy Spirit, who is just like Jesus except that you cannot see him or touch him or hear him speak with a voice like your voice.

Don't you think it would be wonderful to have God come to you and help you believe all the wonderful things that he has to tell you? So do I. Let's pray that the Holy Spirit will come to all of us today.

Dear God, we are tired of looking at the world through dirty glasses. We want you to send us your Spirit so we can see all the people and places the way you want us to see them. Most of all we want to know that you love us, so please send him to us today. Thank you.

THE FAMILY OF GOD

John 10:11-16, vs. 16: And I have other sheep, that are not of this fold; I must bring them also, and they will heed my voice. So there shall be one flock, one shepherd.

Object: A book made up of several sheets of paper folded in half with the names of nations and denominations and races on each page. The front cover should have the picture of the Good Shepherd and the name "The Family of God." When you are telling your story, show only one page at a time, not revealing the title until the end.

Good morning, boys and girls. Someone asked me this morning if he always had to smile when he was in church. Well, I don't know if you always *have* to smile, but I think that my face would rather have me smile than have me any other way. Maybe your face would rather have you frown or do nothing at all, but since I have so many things to be happy about, I just naturally like to smile. I like to smile not only when I'm in church but when I'm other places as well.

Someone also asked me if there were two kinds of crosses in the Christian Church. Well, there are really many kinds of crosses and maybe some day we'll bring in the different kinds. In some churches we see a cross with Jesus on it, while in other churches the cross is empty. Let me explain why. Some people like to think about the great sacrifice that Jesus made for us by dying on the cross. They have a cross that is called a crucifix. Other people like an empty cross because it makes them think about Jesus being risen from the dead, alive and working in the world. Some churches and some people have both.

I'm glad that someone thought to ask me that question, because it helps me to tell the story I wanted to tell you this morning. I brought a book with me that is a do-it-yourself book. When I open this book there are not a lot of words written on each page, but rather there is only one word for each page. Would you like to help me read this book out loud? [*Begin turning the pages, having them repeat the words aloud.*] Nigerians, Presbyterians, Norwegians, Americans, Methodists, White Men, Roman Catholics, Baptists, Germans, French, Lutherans, Episcopalians, Black Men, Yellow Men, Brazilians, Canadians, Mennonites, Mexicans, Red Men, etc.

What a strange book this is for our lesson today! But this book has an important lesson for us to learn. I want you to look at the front cover and tell me who this is and what he is doing. [*Let them answer.*] That's right, Jesus is the Good Shepherd, and we are his sheep. All the people in the world belong to Jesus. He even said in the Bible that there should be one flock and one shepherd. He meant that we should all be able to live together as one people. All of us may have different names or live in different countries and have different color skin, but he wants us all to be one. We can be German sheep or white sheep or Lutheran sheep, but when he asks us who is our shepherd and to whom we all belong, we must be ready to answer. Jesus is our Good Shepherd and we are all Christians.

Look at the cover of this book and read what it says: "The Family of God." If I took one page out of this book I would be taking away part of the family of God. Everybody in this book and every place in this book and every color in this book was made by God and belongs to God. We must be very careful to keep it the way God made it and be very happy that we have such a good God and such a Good Shepherd to take care of us. Remember "The Family of God" book and never forget that all of his people belong to him and that we are very grateful that he included a place in his world for us.

MAKING A CHOICE

John 16:16-22, vs. 20: Truly, truly, I say to you, you will weep and lament but the world will rejoice; you will be sorrowful, but your sorrow will turn into joy.

Object: Some dental equipment and, if possible, some demonstration teeth that would be used in a dental hygiene clinic for school children.

It certainly is good to see you here this morning, worshipping God and sharing with your friends the good time we have here. I want to talk to you about a very important group in our church called the choir. What does the choir do? They sing, that's right. Did you know that when the choir was first used in worship the choir people did *all* the singing and the rest of the people just listened? The choir took the part of the congregation and learned all the music. Choirs are not like that anymore. As a matter of fact, the most important job for a choir today is not the singing of special music but leading the people in their singing. The choir helps other people enjoy singing and speaking during the service.

Speaking of helping, I brought along some things that I got from a good friend of yours. First of all, I brought Terry Teeth with me. The dentist gave Terry to me to show you what you need to know. Let's imagine that Terry has a small cavity right here. [*Using a marking pencil, draw a black area on the teeth to illustrate.*] Now the cavity doesn't hurt yet, but when you see your friend the dentist, he tells you that the cavity has to be fixed or you will have a sore mouth. You must now ask yourself whether you want to have the tooth fixed while it is a little cavity, or whether you want to wait until the pain comes and perhaps even have to have the tooth pulled out. Now, I don't suppose that anyone likes to have his teeth fixed in the same way that he likes other things. Why, I think if I asked my friend the dentist, even he would rather go to a ballgame or eat a hotdog than have his teeth fixed. But what are we going to do? Should we wait and keep things the same or should we have our teeth fixed? While you are thinking about that, let me give you another problem.

After Jesus had risen from the grave and was living again, spending part of his time with the disciples, he said to them that he was going to have to leave again. This time it would be for good. The disciples were very sad and told him that they never wanted him to leave again. But Jesus said if he stayed with them he would not be able to go back to his Father in heaven and make things ready for them and for all people when they were ready to spend their new life with God. Besides, Jesus said, the rest of the people in the world would never know about him and all the wonderful things he has for them if he did not leave them and go. Now I ask you, what do you think Jesus should have done? Should he have stayed with the disciples and lived only in the Holy Land? Or are you glad that he went back to heaven where he could not only live with his Father but also share himself with all people? [*Let them answer if they will.*] I see that you are glad he went back to heaven, even if it meant that the disciples were sad for a little while.

What would you rather do, have a cavity and wait until you have a toothache, or have it fixed now and never have a toothache? I see that you would much rather have it fixed now. That is the way Jesus felt. He said the disciples would be sorry for a little while but everybody else would be happy if he went back to heaven where he could spend time with everybody rather than just with a few friends. Jesus went back to heaven where he will be with all of us in our new life in heaven.

THE BIG ADVANTAGE

John 16:4b-13a, vs. 7: Nevertheless I tell you the truth: it is to your advantage that I go away, for if I do not go away, the Counsellor will not come to you; but if I go, I will send him to you.

Object: A lever or a wrench and, depending upon which you use, some very heavy weight or a bolt fastened too tightly for a child to unscrew with his fingers.

Good morning, boys and girls. I was looking over some ideas in my Bible this week to see what special thing I could tell you. Did you know that the Bible is more than just one book? It is a whole library of books, for there are 66 books in the Bible. Some of the books are very long, while others may only be one page long. The Bible is a very important book, the most important book in the whole world. Someone once asked me if I had an advantage with God because I read my Bible so much. Do you know what the word *advantage* means? It's a very special word, and one that I think we should talk about.

I will need some strong volunteers for this experiment. [*Choose several children.*] My, these are certainly strong young people we have chosen today. Do you see these boxes? I want all of you to see if you can lift these boxes so that the bottom box gets at least one side off the floor. You can't do it? [*Take your lever or crowbar or a one-by-one and pry it up until the boxes are off the floor on one side.*] See, that wasn't very hard, was it? Let me see you try again. Will one of you see if you can unscrew this bolt for me? None of you can do that either? Well, let me show you. [*Now use your wrench.*] See how easy that was when you have the *advantage*? My advantage was having the right tools to do the job. I can do things that you cannot do when I have the advantage. Do you understand? The reason I'm telling you this is that we must have all the help we can get if we're to do certain jobs. Maybe if I worked real hard and took all day I could unscrew that bolt with my bare hands, but I probably could not. With one little wrench I can do it in a second. We need the advantage of a wrench.

Now you are wondering what this has to do with Jesus. Perhaps you will remember a week or so ago I told you that Jesus wanted to go back to heaven to be with his Father. In today's lesson he not only told us that he wanted to go back, but also that it would be to our *advantage* if he went. He said that when he went back to heaven he would send the Holy Spirit, the Counsellor, to us.

What advantage do we have with Jesus in heaven and the Holy Spirit here that we would not have if Jesus were here? There are a lot of things that are better, but a couple of them are these: Jesus said that the Holy Spirit will help us believe things that without him we could not believe. Jesus said that we can ask for things in his name and that he will see that we get them. All we have to do is pray and Jesus will answer our prayers. You see, we have a tremendous advantage with Jesus in heaven and the Holy Spirit here helping us to believe. We have the biggest advantage that people have ever had. We should take advantage of what Jesus has done for us and be grateful that he worked it out this way.

ASKING IN JESUS' NAME

John 16:23b-30, vs. 24: Hitherto you have asked nothing in my name; ask and you will receive, that your joy may be full.

Object: Things that identify a name: tongue depressor -- doctor; money changer or newspaper bag -- paper boy; stole -- pastor; policeman's badge -- policeman, etc.

Wouldn't it be wonderful if some morning I said "Good morning" to everyone and used your names? Good morning, Carol; Good morning, John," etc. But we never seem to have enough time. Names are important. Do you know what the name Jesus means? There used to be a lot of people who had the name Jesus, but it is not a common name today. A long time ago people used the name as they use John or James today, and then they would very often tell who the father was or what town the person was from. For instance, they called Jesus "Jesus, son of Joseph," and "Jesus of Nazareth." Names are important. Jesus means "God's salvation," which is exactly what He means for us.

Sometimes all we have to do is see something and right away we think of somebody and what he does. For instance, if I took this piece of wood and asked you to open your mouth real wide, who would you think of right away? [*Let them answer.*] Very good, the doctor. How about this one? [*Newspaper bag.*] That's right, a paper boy. Let's try one more and see if you are still as sharp. [*The badge.*] Right again. When you see one of these things you immediately think of a person who uses it and that reminds you of someone's name like Dr. Jones or newsboy John or Patrolman McCarthy.

There is something else to think about also. If you need a newspaper to read, you don't go to the doctor, do you? Of course not. You would say, "John, I want a newspaper. Can you help me?" And he would. He would see that you got the newspaper you wanted. That's what Jesus wants you and me to do with him. Jesus says that when we have something to ask of God, whether it be for his help, his love or peace, we should ask it in Jesus' name and we will get it. You can't read John, but John will get the newspaper for you to read. Well, Jesus isn't medicine, but he can help you when you are sick to get the right medicine. And Jesus isn't a road sign, but he can help you when you feel lost.

Do you understand what I mean? If you need something, ask God in the name of Jesus and he will see that what is best for you will happen. And don't forget his name: we call him Jesus, which means "God's salvation." Jesus is God's way of helping us when we are in need.

HAPPY BIRTHDAY!

John 15:26-16:4a, vs. 4a: But I have said these things to you, that when their hour comes you may remember that I told you of them.

Object: A birthday card [or cards for each child].

Some days are very important to all of us, like the day that school lets out every year, or the day that the family begins its vacation, or even the fourth of July. Sometimes the day is so important that we give it a very special name, like Easter or Christmas. How many of you remember what happened on Easter that makes it such an important day? That's right, it is the day that Jesus came back to life from the dead. That was very good, but let's see how you do with another one, like Christmas. Who remembers what happened on Christmas? That's right, Jesus was born. We have made it a day that no one will ever forget.

Speaking of birthdays, let me show you something that I brought with me. I know all of you have seen these before. [*Show the big birthday card.*] What is this? A birthday card. You know, some time ago, before you were even born, your mother went to the doctor and he told her that she was going to have a baby. Your mother was very happy. One of the first questions she asked the doctor was, "When is the baby going to be born?" The doctor was able to tell her what day it would be. Now he may have said July 26 or April 5 or July 20 or May 10, but he gave her one day and he told her that the baby was going to be born on that day. Sure enough, on that day or almost that day, a baby was born to that mother and that baby was you! Whenever that day comes each year we stop and remember it with gifts and cards just like this to show you and everybody else how important that day that you were born on is.

Jesus told us some things that were going to happen.

He said that he wanted us to remember that he had said these things so that when they happened we would remember him. You see, Jesus knows everything there is to know about us and the world that we live in. When he says that something is going to happen, it happens. But the important thing about Jesus is not that he can tell the future but that he cares about what happens to us in the future. You see, the important thing about the doctor was not that he can tell your mother on what day you were going to be born. The important thing that the doctor did was to take good care of your mother and you before you were born. That's the way it is with Jesus and his people. There are some things that we just know are going to happen when we are Christians and a lot of those things are told to us in the Bible. But that is not so important as the fact that before, during and after these things happen, Jesus is always there loving and caring for us.

I want you to remember how important some days are for us as Christians. One of the most important days is our birthday, for that is when God gave us life and made us special persons for his kingdom.

JESUS KNOWS

John 14:23-31a, vs. 29: And now I have told you before it takes place, so that when it does take place, you may believe.

Object: A baseball bat.

Good morning, my young friends. Let me tell you how good it is to see you here on this beautiful spring day. It has been fifty days since Jesus came back from the dead. Fifty days since Easter, and we give this day a very special name, *Pentecost.* Did you know that something we all love very much was born on this day? That's right, many years ago today the Church was born, and it has lived a wonderful life. Maybe we should sing Happy Birthday to the Church. [*Sing if desired.*] That was great!

It is good to remember the Church and thank God for all that has happened during its lifetime. I have something else to remember with you this morning. A long time ago there was a great baseball player by the name of Babe Ruth. How many of you have ever heard of Babe Ruth? A lot of you. He was the greatest ballplayer who ever lived, and one day in the World Series he came to bat near the end of the game. The people were rooting for the other team, and they really cheered when the pitcher threw two strikes to Babe Ruth. Then the Babe took his bat and pointed to the wall in center field and on the next pitch he hit a home run right where he said he would.

It really is great when we do the things that we say we can do. Jesus was like that. He told the disciples a lot of things that were going to happen and they all came true. When they happened the disciples remembered that Jesus had told them about these things days before or even months before, and they believed that Jesus knew everything.

44

When Babe Ruth hit that home run everyone thought he was wonderful, but even Babe Ruth could only do that once in a while. Jesus would tell people what was going to happen so that they would believe that he was sent from God and he was right every time. That is because Jesus is the Son of God, and God knows everything even before it happens. That's one of the reasons, among many, that men believed in Jesus. If you read your Bible you will see how much Jesus knows and how much he can help you if you will listen to what he says.

AUTHORITY

Matthew 28:18-20, vs. 18: And Jesus came and said to them, "All authority in heaven and on earth has been given to me."

Object: Comic strips in which the artist's signature is plain for all of them to see.

Good morning to you, boys and girls. How many of you have ever heard me talk about the Father, Son and Holy Ghost? You have? Do you know what that means? There is only one God, right? Right. But we know God in three different ways. We know God as a Father, as a Son and as the Holy Ghost. How can one God be three persons? See if this helps. How many people am I? Just one, that's right. Now when I am talking to my wife, I am a husband. When I am playing with my children, I am their father. When I am listening to my father, I am his son. [*This may take some careful conversation, explaining relationships, etc.*] You see, I am different persons to different people, but I am only one. Well, now, that isn't exactly the way it is with God, but it helps us to understand how one God can be three persons.

I know that you believe that Jesus Christ is God and because he is God he is powerful. He has authority. Do you know what *authority* means? That's a big word. But there is a smaller word in it. Let me show you what I mean. Do you know what I brought with me this morning? [*Hold up the comic strips.*] How many of you read the comics? Good. Are they real people like you and me? No. Who makes them for the comics? Well, right here in each comic strip the man who makes the drawings of the people signs his name. We call him an *author*. That's the little word in the big word *authority*.

Jesus says that he is the author of the heavens and the earth. That means he made it and he is in charge. He made us and he is in charge of us. Jesus has and is authority and

46

we are glad. It is good that Jesus is in charge.

The man in the comics can have his people laugh and run and jump. He draws the comic strip. Jesus is our author and he can make us happy and full and joy and love. We need to listen to our author, Jesus, and to what he says, for he is in charge.

GOD'S WARNING

Luke 16:19-31, vss. 27, 28: And he said, "Then I beg you, father, to send him to my father's house, for I have five brothers, so that he may warn them, lest they also come into this place of torment."

Object: A package of cigarettes with the warning "Caution: Smoking may be hazardous to your health."

This week we celebrate Memorial Day. While Memorial Day is a holiday for people like you and me, it is also kind of a warning. Memorial Day tells us about all of the men who died as soldiers fighting for their country. It is a warning about what happens when men cannot solve their problems by talking and listening. When they can't, they start fighting and the fighting gets worse until someone dies. We always pray that each war will be the last one ever fought, but somehow we forget and others forget the warning of how horrible war is for people.

Warnings are important. But many times people don't listen to warnings. Let me show you what I mean. Here is something that all of you have seen. What is in this package? Cigarettes, that's right. One the side of every package are printed some words. Would you like to read the words aloud? [*Ask an older child to read them.*] That's what it says. It could be very bad for your health, and make you very sick. Now I know that a lot of people smoke cigarettes even though they are warned not to, but there are other even more important warnings which many people don't heed.

For instance, God tells us how to live, to be kind and share what we have with others. God says don't be angry or hate each other. Don't steal or lie or kill because if you do things are going to be bad for you. This is a warning God says to every man, woman and child. But people think, "God doesn't mean me. He must be warning the other people, but not me."

Well, God does mean me, and you and you and you. He means that his warning is for everybody. And you know, God is saying that a warning isn't bad. As a matter of fact, God says you will be happier if you don't do the bad things. People would be happy if they did not smoke, for even the people who do smoke wish they did not. The same thing is true about God's warnings. People who lie wish they didn't. They all wish they loved and cared for other people and obeyed God's warning.

THERE'S ALWAYS ROOM IN HEAVEN

Luke 14:15-24, vs. 22: And the servant said, "Sir, what you commanded has been done, and still there is room."

Object: A suitcase and a lot of clothes.

Good morning to every child who can tell me what month this is. JUNE, that's right! And what is special about June? Did you know that June is the month when a lot of people get married? Is there anyone here who wants to get married?

June is also the month when we start our vacations. How many of you are happy that school is out? Almost all of you. Well, I brought with me something that goes with vacations. How many of you know what this is? [*Hold up the suitcase.*] That's right, a suitcase. And do you know what I am going to do? I am going to show you how this suitcase is like heaven. That's right!

One of the things that always makes me unhappy is when people talk about how hard it is to get into heaven. But, you know, it isn't hard at all. Some people make you think that God doesn't want a whole lot of people in heaven, but only a very few. That isn't true either. God wants everybody to live with him forever and he has made a place big enough for everybody. Let me show you what I mean.

Take a look at this suitcase. Let's pretend it is heaven and these clothes are people. Now there are a lot of clothes here and we are going to put them in one at a time. Now, every time I put in a pair of socks, or a shirt, or a necktie, I still have room for more. That's the way God's heaven is, only it is a huge suitcase. It is the biggest suitcase for people that there ever was. And God keeps calling his people out of this world into his big "suitcase" called heaven and still there is room for more.

I don't want one boy or one girl ever to worry if there is room for him in God's heaven, because there always will be room. You just remember that in God's heaven there is always room for more people, just as there is room in my suitcase for all my vacation clothes.

THE CHRISTIAN'S ROAD MAP

Luke 15:1-10, vs. 7: Even so, I tell you, there will be more joy in heaven over one sinner who repents than over the ninety-nine righteous persons who need no repentance.

Object: A road map.

Good morning, boys and girls. Do you all know where you are? Are you sure that none of you is lost? That's good. Has anyone here ever been lost? Isn't that an awful feeling?

I remember one time when I was lost. I thought I knew where I was going and it was the wrong direction. Before long there were fewer and fewer houses, and the couple of houses that I did see had no one living in them. The sun started going down and the trees seemed very tall and made dark shadows across the road. Pretty soon the clouds in the sky got darker and darker and I thought it was going to rain. All I could see was a long road in front of me and some fields with weeds in them beside me. I was really afraid. Then I remembered something that I had almost forgotten about. In my glove compartment in the car was a road map. I opened the little door and took it out. Pretty soon I knew that if I turned around and went back the way I had come and then followed my map I would soon be where I wanted to go. I would be safe and unafraid. That good old map showed me the way to get where I wanted to go.

You know, the Bible is like a road map for Christians. All of us get lost sometimes, and we keep right on going in the wrong direction. Maybe you can remember telling a lie. You had to tell another lie and then another and another to make the first lie sound like the truth. Boy, oh, boy, you thought. I am a long way from the truth and I better get back. But you were afraid because someone would find out that you had lied. Forget it! Go back! The Christian road map teaches us to tell the truth. And we should also learn to say we are sorry to the people we have hurt along the way. Then we know we are going in the right direction and instead of being afraid we are happy.

The Bible is a good road map because God directs us through it. God is much happier with people who know they have done wrong and correct it than he is with people who believe they have never done anything wrong. God likes one who says he is sorry and means it.

CHOOSING OUR TEACHERS

Luke 6:36-42, vs. 39: He also told them a parable. "Can a blind man lead a blind man? Will they not both fall into a pit?"

Object: Two blindfolds.

Good morning, boys and girls. Isn't it fun to get up on Sunday morning and come to church? I think it is. I would like to have a little fun with you this morning if I can. How many of you have a favorite teacher? Oh, a lot of you. Why is this person a favorite teacher? [*Let them answer.*] Those are all good reasons, but let me tell you another reason. I think your favorite teacher is special because this teacher knows so much and helps you to learn, too.

Jesus taught us that we must choose our teachers very carefully because we will be a lot like them. Let me show you what I mean. I need a volunteer. [*Select one and blindfold him.*] That's good. I hope that you can't see out. Very good. Now I am going to select another volunteer and we are going to pretend that this volunteer is your teacher. He is going to lead you wherever you go. O.K.?

Only one thing is wrong. We are going to blindfold your teacher also. Now we will ask him to walk with you and you must follow him. [*Let them move around a little.*] This would be poor teaching, wouldn't it? If the teacher is no better at leading than you are, then neither one of you is going to do very well.

Jesus teaches us to choose our teachers very carefully. They should be people we know and trust. The best teacher, of course, is Jesus, and we must all try to follow his teachings. But Jesus wants us to have good teachers here in our church and in our schools and in our homes. We must always choose people who are good Christians, who show a lot of love for God and for other people.

Remember what happens when we are not careful? We choose people who do not see any better or know any better than we do!

FISHERS OF MEN

Luke 5:1-11, vs. 10b: And Jesus said to Simon, "Do not be afraid; henceforth you will be catching men."

Object: Some gold fish or any pet fish.

Good morning, children. Isn't it great to join your Christian friends this morning in worshipping God? A long time ago Jesus and his friends were resting by the sea and he was teaching people from a boat which was anchored a little way out in the water. After he had finished teaching he told the disciples, who were tired from fishing all night, to go out a little further and put their nets into the water.

Now, Jesus had a special reason for telling them this. Although they didn't want to do it, they knew better than to argue too much with Jesus. Peter, James, Andrew and John were all fishermen. I suppose they were about the best fishermen I have ever heard about, and most of the time they liked to fish. I brought some fish with me this morning. [*Hold up your fish bowl.*] These are pretty small fish; they are not the kind that the disciples fished for, but we can pretend they were like this only much bigger.

Well, these fish had stayed out of Peter's, James', John's and Andrew's nets all night, which is really the best time to fish. But when Jesus told them to put down their nets they caught more fish than they could handle. Maybe that's where my little fishes' great grandfathers were caught and put in a bowl. Anyway, the disciples were so amazed at all of these fish and the size of them that they just fell down and praised God.

But do you know what Jesus said? He said, "Men, what you have caught today is nothing compared to what you are *going* to catch. Today you caught fish, but tomorrow you are going to catch men."

He didn't mean that they would be catching men in a net and putting them in a bowl. Jesus meant that they were going to be ministers and teachers and missionaries for Jesus. They would be "catching" men, bring them to God.

That's what it means to be a disciple of Jesus. You don't use nets, you use God's word and you help people learn about Jesus. That's what Jesus meant when he told the disciples that they would be fishers of men.

GOD'S BANDAGE

Matthew 5:20-26, vss. 23, 24: So if you are standing before the altar in the Temple, offering a sacrifice to God, and suddenly remember that a friend has something against you, leave your sacrifice there beside the altar and go and be reconciled to him and then come and offer your sacrifice to God.

Object: A bandage.

Good morning, everyone. I hope this is a good day for you. Things are almost always good for you, aren't they? I suppose that the only really bad times you have are when you get hurt while playing. Is that right? Has anyone been hurt this summer? [*Let them respond . . . look for leg or arm cuts.*] Boy, that must have really hurt! Did you cry? I suppose if it was that serious you had to quit playing. [*Now work for the answer that they had to stop what they were doing and go home to be fixed up.*] If you had to quit playing because of the cut, I suppose you went home to be helped. What kind of help do you get for a cut like that? Do you ever have to use a bandage? I thought so. By putting some medicine and a bandage on it we know that it soon will be better and then we can start playing again. Right?

Well, God said that sometimes we need to use another kind of medicine that will help fix us up just like the bandage we use when we are hurt. Let me tell you what I mean. Sometimes we think about going to church on Sunday, but we remember that we have had a bad fight with one of our friends. It may even have been his fault because he started it. Still, we really hurt because we are not friends anymore. God says we need a bandage -- a special kind of bandage that will help us to stop hurting. This bandage is called "forgiving love." When we go to our friend and tell him that we are sorry and that we don't want to fight anymore, then our hurt begins to feel a lot better. God then says when we have used that kind of a bandage on ourselves we should come to church and he will make us completely healthy again.

Do you know what I am talking about? You remember when you had a fight or an argument with your friend and how badly you felt. Just think how good it would have been if you had gone and told him that you were sorry that it ever happened. That's called *reconciling*. That's a big word, but that's God's medicine for making peace here on earth.

Now the next time you see a bandage, remember that God wants you to make peace with all who are not happy with you.

THE "SORRY" PEOPLE

Mark 8:1-9, vs. 2: I have compassion on the crowd, because they have been with me now three days, and have nothing to eat.

Object: A gas can and car window cleaner.

Good morning to all of you boys and girls. Who can tell me what day it is today? Sunday, that's right, and what a tremendous day this Sunday is going to be. When you got up this morning did you take a deep breath and thank God for being alive and well? I hope so!

I want to talk to you this morning about a word that is very easy to use. The word is *sorry*. I'm sorry. I'm sorry that I broke it. I am really sorry. I'm sorry that I hurt you. I'm sorry that I forgot. I'm sorry, sorry, sorry! Some people are always sorry but that's all they are. We call them the sorry people.

Let me show you what I mean. One day I was driving along the road and I ran out of gas. Somebody came along and stopped and said, "I'm sorry you ran out of gas." And then he drove on. He was sorry that I was out of gas but he didn't do anything about it. Another time I pulled into a service station and the man said that he was sorry that my windows were dirty. And then he just went right on with what he was doing. If these people really cared they would have gotten me some what for my car when it wouldn't go? [*Hold up gas can.*] That's right, gasoline. Or the man who told me my windows were dirty should have done what? [*Hold up the window cleaner.*] That's right, he would have cleaned my windows.

Well, Jesus was not like that. One day he said that a lot of people were hungry and would soon get sick if they didn't get something to eat. He could have said to them, "I'm sure sorry that you are hungry," because he really was. But he did more than that; he fed them. He gave them bread and fish. That's something for all of us to remember. Whenever we can do more than just feel sorry for people who are in trouble or have need, we should do so. That means you really have *compassion*. That's a big word that means that you are not just sorry -- you are going to *do* something about it!

GOOD FRUIT... GOOD PEOPLE

Matthew 7:15-21, vs. 20: Yes, the way to identify a tree, or a person, is by the kind of fruit produced.

Object: A good apple and a rotten apple.

Good morning, boys and girls. Have you ever noticed how you can tell what kind of a person someone is by the things that he does? Do you know what I mean? A person who is mean does mean things, and a good person does good things.

Have you ever seen one of these before? [*Hold up the good apple.*] An apple! How about this apple? [*Hold up the one with rotten spots or worm holes.*] Do you think that they came from the same tree? No, they didn't, did they? This apple came from a tree in an orchard where the tree was very well cared for every day of the year. The branches were trimmed, the leaves were sprayed, the fruit was picked at just the right time. But this poor apple just grew wild with no one to care for it. It finally fell to the ground where it started to rot. You can't fool the people about which apple they want to eat. People want to have the good apple that comes from the good tree.

People are like these apples. People who know and are close to God, Jesus says, are well taken care of because God can use his love on them. They listen to his laws, try to obey them, know of his love and use it not only for themselves but for others as well.

People who live by themselves and for themselves are like the apple that grows wild. Pretty soon they do mean things, they forget about other people and they care only for themselves. Jesus says that you can tell about people just as you can tell about trees. If people do good things for others they are people who share God's love. If they are mean we can tell that they do not know of God.

62

Think about the difference between the good and the bad fruit the next time you eat a big, juicy apple. Then remember that there can be two kinds of people, too. It's up to you to decide which kind you will be.

A POOR MIXTURE

Luke 16:1-9 or 15:11; 32, vs. 31: "Look, son dear," his father said to him, "you and I are very close and everything I have is yours. But it is right to celebrate. For he is your brother; and he was dead and has come back to life! He was lost and is found."

Object: Water colors of blue and yellow which, when mixed, make green.

Good morning, boys and girls. This morning we are going to have an experiment for artists. How many of you like to paint? Oh, boy, almost all of you. Well, I have with me today two colors. One of these colors is my very favorite of all colors. Can you guess which one of these is my favorite? [*Hold up blue and yellow.*] How many say blue? How many say yellow? My favorite is blue, and I love to paint with it. [*Put some blue paint on the paper.*] Isn't that a pretty color? How many of you know what would happen if I would paint over my blue color with yellow? Do you think it would stay blue? No? Do you think it would be yellow? Let's see. [*Paint it over the blue until it turns green.*] Oh, my, it isn't either blue or yellow at all! It's green. Blue and yellow make green.

There is a good reason why I have shown you this experiment. Boys and girls can be like colors, too. Did you know that? The nicest boy or girl can change to the meanest and ugliest boy and girl you ever saw by adding one thing called jealousy.

Jesus told us about a man who had two sons. One of the sons left home with all his possessions. After he was gone for a short time he lost or spent everything he had. So he went back home. The son who stayed home was afraid that when his brother returned the father would take away some of the things that belonged to him and give them to his brother. In fact, he didn't like the idea of his brother's coming home at all. It made him very jealous. In fact, it turned him from a good man into an ugly man.

We are jealous when we are afraid that something that belongs to us is going to belong to someone else. When we are jealous we are not as pretty or good as we were before. When we add yellow to blue we get green. When we add jealousy to boys and girls we get hate and ugliness. So make sure you are not like the one brother, but always be willing to share what has been given to you and never be jealous of anyone.

A TIME FOR EVERYTHING

Luke 19:41-47a: *They will bring you to the ground, you and your children within your walls, and not leave you one stone standing on another, because you did not recognize God's moment when it came.*

Object: A tooth brush and tooth paste.

Good morning, boys and girls. Tell me what day it is today. Sunday, that's right. Can you tell me what the date is? It's August, isn't it, but what day? Some of you know, but a lot of you forget. It's easy to forget things, isn't it?

Let me show you something that lots of boys and girls forget when their mothers and fathers don't remind them. [*Hold up tooth brush and tooth paste.*] Does anyone here ever forget to brush his teeth? You do? Boy, that's pretty serious, isn't it? If you forget one day, you may not have too much trouble. But if you forget for too many days, what happens? Cavities! Oh, me, oh, my! The next thing you know you might have a toothache and then you really have problems. Of course, we know that we should not only brush our teeth but we should also go to the dentist at least twice a year for a check-up. When we forget that we only invite trouble.

A long time ago Jesus stood high on a hill and looked down on Jerusalem and he cried. Not the kind of crying that might happen when we scratch a knee or have a fight. Jesus cried because he felt so sorry for the people of Jerusalem who had forgotten all that God had taught them and who missed knowing Jesus as the Son of God. That's right, the people were so busy doing what they thought was important that they missed knowing Jesus for who he really was.

We should brush our teeth but we forget because we think we have something more important to do. We end up with cavities and a toothache. Just so, people make themselves too busy and pass up Jesus and end up very

66

unhappy and disappointed.

There is a time for everything, including a time to brush our teeth and a time to listen and worship God.

WHO IS WORTH MORE?

Luke 18:9-14, vs. 14: It was this man, I tell you, and not the other, who went home acquitted of his sins. For everyone who exalts himself will be humbled, and whoever humbles himself will be exalted.

Object: A fifty-cent piece and a dime.

Good morning, boys and girls. I want to tell you a story about two friends of mine, Harley Half-Dollar and Dimmy the Dime. Now I call them both my friends, but let me show you why one of them means a little more to me than the other.

One day I picked up Harley Half-Dollar and Dimmy Dime and put them in my pocket. On the way to where I was going I could hear them talking -- I should say I heard Harley talking. Harley said, "Oh, Dimmy, I don't know why you hang around. You're not worth anything. What can anyone buy for a dime? You can't buy a Sunday newspaper, a double dip ice cream cone, a chocolate sundae, or take someone to a movie. Dimmy, you are hardly worth anything. Now take me. I'm worth 50 cents and I can buy several comic books, a strawberry soda, a ride on a pony -- maybe even two; why I can do anything that you can do five times better."

Poor Dimmy. He just fell farther and farther down in my pocket until he was right in the bottom corner. "What can you do, Dimmy," asked Harley. Dimmy very quietly said, "I'll do whatever my friend asks me to do that only costs ten cents." "Ha, ha," laughed Harley, "you'll probably spend the rest of your days in a pocket while I'm out seeing the world."

Just then we all three arrived where we were going and I reached into my pocket, pulled out one of my friends, and put him into the slot in the telephone. That's right, still deep in my pocket was the very surprised and deflated friend, Harley Half-Dollar, and beginning his trip around the world was Dimmy the Dime.

Now Jesus once taught the same thing about people. He said that people who think too much about themselves usually get their feelings hurt. But people who think of others first, before themselves, will have many happy things happen to them. That's the way it was with Harley and Dimmy. Harley just thought about himself and he's still in my pocket. But Dimmy only looked for ways to help others and he's on his way around the world.

THE BIG DIFFERENCE

Mark 7:31-37, vs. 37: Their astonishment knew no bounds; "All that he does, he does well," they said; "he even makes the deaf hear and the dumb speak."

Object: Some paper and crayons and a beautiful picture. If you have an artist in the congregation here is the opportunity to use him. You must both work on the announced theme.

Good morning to you, boys and girls. How many of you like to color or draw? Almost all of you. Well, I do, too, and I thought this morning I would like to draw something for you. How about a horse or a tree? Why not both? Well, let's see. [*If you use an artist, here is the place to introduce him and announce that both of you will be drawing the same pictures.*]

While I'm doing this, let me talk to you a little bit about Jesus. Did you know that one day when he was out with his friends, the disciples, they met a man who could not hear or speak? People must have liked this man very much and they also felt very sorry for him. Now lots of people had tried to help. They probably helped him hear by listening for loud noises and pushing him out of the way so he wouldn't get hurt, or by going to the store and speaking for him and telling the owner what he wanted to buy. They must have done a pretty good job.

But when they brought him to Jesus they expected Jesus to do more than they could do. Well, do you know what? He did. He healed this man so that he could hear and speak. But even though they expected a lot, Jesus did this so well that the people were just flabbergasted.

How do you like my drawing of my horse and tree? Pretty good? I have another drawing here done by another artist. Would you like to see it? [*If you have an artist, here is where you show his work.*] Which one do you like better? Well, you see, that's the way it is with ordinary men and Jesus. We can do things pretty well most of the time, but when Jesus did something, it was super. It's kind of like comparing my drawing with the artist's drawing. There really is a difference, don't you think? Well, there really is a difference between man and God, too. When we do things they are all right, but when God does something, it is *super!*

KNOWING AND DOING

Luke 10:23-37, vss. 26-28: Jesus said, "What is written in the law? What is your reading of it?" He replied, "Love the Lord your God with all your heart, with all your soul, with all your strength, and with all your mind; and your neighbor as yourself." "That is the right answer," said Jesus. "Do that and you will live."

Object: A physician's prescription and a bottle of medicine.

Good morning, boys and girls. This morning I have a riddle for you. But before I ask you the riddle, I want to tell you a story. A long time ago people used to try to ask Jesus very hard questions to see if he really knew what he was talking about. For instance, one day he was asked if it was possible to live forever. Jesus answered, "You can read the Bible. What does the Bible say?" The man who had asked the question told him what the Bible said, and Jesus then looked him right in the eye and said, "Now that you know what the Bible says, do it and you will have more than just an answer to a question. You will also have your life forever."

I wanted to show you what Jesus meant so I went to a doctor and told him I had a bad stomachache. He examined my tummy and then he wrote out a prescription for me. [*Hold up your prescription.*] I took the prescription to the drugstore and gave it to the pharmacist. He made some medicine and put it in a bottle. [*Hold up a bottle.*] I took the medicine home, got a drink of water and took the medicine.

Now, my riddle is this: When did I start getting well? When I went to the doctor? When he wrote the prescription? When I went to the drugstore? When he made the medicine? When I went home? Or was it when I took the medicine with the drink of water? [*Let them answer.*]

To get well, I needed to do all of those things, didn't I? I started getting well by going to the doctor. Yet it wouldn't have helped a bit until I took my first pill.

That's what Jesus told the man about having life forever. You might begin by knowing what the Bible tells you, but until you *do* what it says, it is just like not knowing anything. We must know God and what he says, and then *do* what God tells us to do.

PRAISING GOD LOUDLY

Luke 17:11-19, vs. 15: One of them, finding himself cured, turned back praising God loudly.

Object: A cheerleader's megaphone or some piece of equipment that will amplify the speaking voice.

[*Begin by using the megaphone.*] GOOD MORNING, BOYS AND GIRLS. HOW ARE YOU TODAY? CAN YOU HEAR ME? OF COURSE YOU CAN! ISN'T THIS EXCITING? HAVE YOU EVER SEEN SOMEONE USE ONE OF THESE? YOU HAVE? WHERE? AT A FOOTBALL GAME? [*Still using the megaphone, give a cheer or the start of one.*] FIGHT, TEAM, FIGHT! WE ALL GET INTO THE FUN THIS WAY, DON'T WE?

Now I think that worship is exciting, too. Worship does not always have to be so quiet. A long time ago when a man was cured by Jesus, the Bible says that he praised God loudly. People heard him because he praised God with a loud voise. They heard him and they got excited.

I think that it would be fun and that God would like to hear us praise him with a loud voice. Let's all see what it would be like to break our silence. I will tell you what to say and then we will all say it together. Are you ready? *"Praise God."* [*Let them repeat it.*] That's great. Isn't it fun? When we do it this way, just look at the enthusiasm. Pretty soon we can sing together, pray together, and even read together with real enthusiasm.

Let's try one. First we will say, "Praise to the Lord" and "Jesus Christ, our King of Glory." Then we can sing a song about God. How would you like to sing "Jesus Loves Me"? [*Or choose any song you wish.*] Let's sing it with a loud and beautiful voice.

Christianity does not mean being quiet all the time. We can also be enthusiastic. That's what the man was when he came back and praised God with a loud voice after Jesus healed him. He was filled with real joy, and he

wanted people to know it. We hope you feel the same way
when Jesus shows you his love.

WORRYING WON'T HELP

Matthew 6:24-34, vs. 27: Is there a man of you who by anxious thought can add a foot to his height?

Object: A wooden box, a long choir robe, a tall hat, and a tape measure.

Good morning to all of you. How are you on this first Sunday in September? Good. Is everybody happy about the idea of school starting? I knew that you were, but I thought that I would just check for the teacher and tell her how much you like it.

Do any of you ever worry about school? Do you worry if you are going to pass or worry about a test or just worry because you like to worry? Jesus used to like to laugh a lot, and one day he said to some people who liked to worry about things that it sure seemed strange to him why people worried. He said that some people worry so much that it makes them sick. Now there are some things that just happen and they are supposed to happen and there is nothing that we can do to change them.

We are going to see if Jesus was really right. First of all, I need four volunteers who would like to be taller than they are now. We are going to try some experiments and see if we can make them taller. [*Select the four and measure them with the tape and tell them to remember how tall they are.*] Now we are going to try to make this one taller by having him stand on a box and maybe he will get so used to standing up there that when we take the box away, he will be as tall as he thinks. To the next one we will give a big choir robe and have him put it on so that if he wears big clothes he might get big enough to walk and play in them. To the third person we are going to give a tall hat with the hope that while we are doing something else his head will just fill it up and then he will be as tall without the hat as he was with it. We are going to stretch the fourth person and see if we can make him any taller.

Now let's see how we made out. Have any of our volunteers grown while we were doing these things to them? [*Take the measuring tape out and remeasure them.*] No, the box didn't work, nor did the hat, nor the choir robe. Let's see if the one we stretched is any taller. No, he is the same size also.

Has anybody worried a lot about these people growing taller while we worked on them? Some people like to worry and they worry about the funniest things. But worry won't work any better than standing on boxes, wearing big clothes or even being stretched. Things like growing up happen according to the plan of God, and nothing that we worry about helps at all.

The next time you get to worrying, think about what Jesus taught us. Remember that God takes care of us just as he does the birds in the air and the grass on the ground.

GOD CARES FOR US

Luke 7:11-16, vs. 16: Deep awe fell upon them all and they praised God. "A great prophet has arisen among us," they said, and again, "God has shown his care for his people."

Object: a first aid kit with a red cross marked on it.

Once in a while, boys and girls, something happens that makes us realize that we really need God's care. Sometimes people begin to think that God really doesn't care what happens to them at all. They say, "What's the use," or they say, "Who cares?" If you tell them that God cares, they say, "Who says?"

Well, God does care about people and he teaches people to care about other people. Let me show you a way that God shows us how to care for one another and because he shows us we know that he cares also. How many of you have ever been hurt while you were playing? Does anybody have a bad cut or bruise that someone has had to put a bandage on lately? [*Wait for their replies and examine some of the cuts and scars.*] Oh, those must have really hurt. Who helped you when you were hurt? Your mother or dad? Aren't you glad that they were there so that you could be helped? Suppose this happened to you somewhere else and your mother or father were not near and couldn't help. What do you think would have happened? Do you think that someone else would have helped?

Look what I brought with me this morning. Does anyone know what we call this box? That's right, a first aid kit. When we look inside it we will find bandages and tape and medicine for cuts and medicine for burns and all sorts of things that help people when they are hurt. A first-aid kit can help people until they can be taken to a doctor if they are really hurt seriously. It is used to take care of the problem right away without having to go home or to the hospital or the doctor's office.

Let's look at one other thing on this first aid kit that I think is really important. Do you see anything on the box that might remind you of Jesus? [*Let them look until they spot the cross.*] That's right, the cross! One of the things that the people knew about God when Jesus came to earth was that God really cared. He cared so much, as a matter of fact, that he died for our sins. If you ever hear anyone say, "Who cares," you can say, "God cares," and I know that it is true because he died for my sins that I may live forever with him. Just as he teaches us to use first aid kits to care for people who are hurt, so he teaches us to care for everyone and everything. One thing is for sure: God cares and he cares a lot!

WATCHING AND LISTENING

Luke 14:1-11, vs. 1: One Sabbath he went to have a meal in the house of a leading Pharisee; and they were watching him closely.

Object: Binoculars, a microscope or a magnifying glass.

Well, this is some day, isn't it? Could you have anything better than a day like this when you can get up in the morning, feel good and be ready to visit with God? Of course not. This is the best place in the whole world to be on a day like this.

How many of you would like to sit down at a table and have Jesus sit down right beside you? We would all like to sit down and eat and talk with Jesus. Suppose he came and ate dinner with you today. How do you think you would act? Some people I know would watch him pretty closely. Let me show you what I mean. Have you ever gone to a football game in which you had to sit way up in the stands to watch the game? Do you remember wishing that you could see the player's face and not just his number? Or have you ever been to a parade and you had to stand in back of so many people that you couldn't really tell who it was who was playing in the band or riding on the float? If you ever wanted to see the things up close that seemed so far away, you could have done it if you had a pair of binoculars. With these you could tell how the player felt after he was tackled. Did he hurt himself or was he laughing or was he angry? Maybe with binoculars you could tell if the person in the band was too hot or cold or whether he thought that he had played a bad note or was walking out of step with the rest of the band. Binoculars let you see things far away better than you can see them with your own eyes.

The reason that I told you this story is that people used to watch Jesus as though they had binoculars on him all the time. Lots of people hoped that he would make a mistake so he would be more like them and less like God. When he went one day to eat at the home of a very important man, the people who did not like Jesus watched him very closely. They watched to see what he ate and how he ate it. They listened to what he said and they watched while he listened to other people. All the time they waited for him to make a mistake. But he never did. Jesus never made a mistake because he was here to show people how God wanted men to live and God doesn't make mistakes. The people learned how it is to be a disciple of God and they changed and tried to be like Jesus.

It is good to watch God closely, so closely that the first thing you know you want to be more like him and less like anybody else. Let's all try to watch and listen to God more closely. Let's pretend that our hands are binoculars [*Hold up your hands to your eyes*] and that we are going to watch Jesus very closely. Then maybe we will be able to become more like him, too.

A PUBLIC OPINION POLL

Matthew 22:34-46, vss. 41, 42: Turning to the assembled Pharisees, Jesus asked them, "What is your opinion about the Messiah? Whose son is he?" "The Son of David," they replied.

Object: A piece of poster board with the words written on it: PUBLIC OPINION POLL with some questions and space for answers to the questions.

This morning we are going to do something that generally only a few big people get to do. We are going to have a Public Opinion Poll and find out how the boys and girls who come to services feel about their church. Now the way that this works is that I will ask each of you a few questions and after each of you gets a chance to answer, we are going to add the answers up.

How do you like the drinking fountains in church?
Are they too high?
Are they too low?
Is the water too cold?
Is the water too warm?
Is the water just right?
How do you like the seats in the church?
Are they too hard?
Are they too straight?
Are they just right?
Can you see everything that you want to see from where you are sitting?
Would you like to sit in the front of the church? The back? The middle?

One last question. This is about the sermon, so be careful how you answer. Do you like to hear the pastor preach? Does he tell good stories? Does he talk too long? Does he talk too fast? Does he talk just to older people?

These are the kinds of questions that are asked in a public opinion poll. To learn how the most people feel I will have to ask all of you some of the questions. [*Ask each child at least one part of the poll if you can't ask him all the questions.*]

Some people think that public opinion polls are brand new, but did you know that Jesus used to have public opinion polls? He did! One day he asked some people what they thought about some questions such as, "What is your opinion about the Messiah? Whose son is he?" Another time he asked his disciples, "Who do the people think I am?" Jesus wanted to know what people thought so that he could speak with them and answer their questions. Jesus knew it was very important to answer our questions about God, and that is why he came and lived on earth.

Opinion polls are not new. They are at least as old as Jesus for he used to take them all the time. Now I am going to take the answers that you gave me this morning and study them. That way I will know how I can best serve and teach you every Sunday.

THE POWER OF GOD

Matthew 9:1-8, vs. 6: But that you may know that the Son of man has authority on earth to forgive sins, he then said to the paralytic -- "Rise, take up your bed and go home."

Object: Signs of authority: a policeman's badge, a nurse's cap.

Good morning, everybody. Isn't this a wonderful day? Here we are all together in church, ready to worship God and make friends with God's people. I have with me this morning some things that belong to some of God's people. I am hoping that you will be able to tell me what these people do.

First of all, I need two helpers, a boy and a girl, so that I can show you what this is all about. [*Choose two volunteers*]. I want to put this on the girl. [*Put on nurse's cap.*] What do you think of when you see someone dressed like this? A nurse, that's right. Where do you see nurses? Right, a hospital. When you go to the hospital, the nurse is in charge. Another way to say it is that she is the *authority*. Whatever she says is the rule.

Let's try another one. Who wears something like this? [*Pin badge on the boy volunteer.*] That's right, a policeman. When the policeman comes around and shows you his badge, you had better listen because he is also an *authority*. Almost all authority has some sign by which you can recognize it.

Jesus was an authority and he also had signs of his authority. One day Jesus told people that he was not pretending about being the Son of Man. To prove that what he said was true, he healed a man who was quite sick, and then he forgave him of his sins.

Ordinary people like you and I have signs like badges and special hats, but Jesus showed that he was the Son of God by forgiving men of their sins and healing them. That made him an authority on God, just as the nurse is about the hospital. Now we know why Jesus healed men. He did so in order that they would know the power of God.

EVERYONE'S WELCOME!

Matthew 22:1-14, vs. 9: Go therefore, to the thorough-fares, and invite to the marriage feast as many as you find.

Object: Baby bottle, cane, crutch, hammer, chalk, apron, Bible, and football helmet.

Good morning, boys and girls. Every once in a while I think it is important to talk about what kind of a kingdom or community God is building. I am afraid that sometimes we may make you think that God is only interested in people who walk around all day with Bibles in their hands and are very quiet. [*Hold Bible under your arm with your hands folded.*] That's not quite true. God does like us to carry our Bibles. But God says that his community is going to be made up of all kinds of people.

Let me show you what kind of a world God is making up for his own. I will hold up an item and you tell me what kind of a person it reminds you of. Let's begin with this. [*Hold up baby bottle.*] A baby! God wants lots of babies in his community. How about this? [*Hold up cane.*] Older people -- grandmothers and grandfathers -- are important in God's world.

And how about this? [*Hold up crutch or thermometer.*] Sick people and ones with broken bones are welcome in God's community. Let's see what other kinds of people God wants. [*Hold up apron, then hammer, then chalk and football helmet.*] That's right, there is a place for mothers and fathers, carpenters, teachers, and football players.

Let's try one or two more. [*Pat your mouth making an Indian's sound, or pull your eyes to a slant like an Oriental.*] That's right, Indians and Chinese and all the peoples of the world are invited by God to be a part of his community. It doesn't make any difference if your skin is red or yellow, black, brown or white -- you are still invited to come and belong to God. The only thing that we must do is get ready and God will make a place for all of us, no matter what we do or how old we are or what we look like. God's place has room for us all, and we are all invited to get ready for his new world.

TWO BY TWO

Luke 10:1-9, vs. 1: After this the Lord appointed seventy others, and sent them on ahead of him, two by two, into every town and place where he himself was about to come.

Object: A pair of shoes, salt and pepper, knife and fork.

Have you ever noticed how certain things go together, boys and girls? For instance, what goes together with boys? Girls! Almost every Sunday morning I say, "Good morning, boys and girls." When I see boys and girls together on Sunday morning, I know that we are going to have a worship service.

The other night I saw two bright lights coming down the road and I knew then what was coming. A car, that's right. Now, let's see what else I have here with me that you might know about. [*Hold up knife and fork.*] What do you call these two things? When you see a knife and fork what does that mean is going to happen? [*Wait for answer.*] You are going to eat! And [*hold up salt and pepper*] what about these? When you see these two friends together what do they mean to you? You put salt and pepper on potatoes, meat, green beans and tomatoes. When you see them you know what is coming, don't you? One more try. [*Hold up basketball shoes.*] What do you call this pair of shoes? Gym shoes, that's right, and when someone wears this kind of shoes you know that he is playing some kind of game. All these pairs, the knife and fork, the salt and pepper and the gym shoes, tell us something else besides what they are. They tell us what to expect.

The reason for this story is that Jesus once had some pairs of people whom he used in a special way. He chose people to go out together in pairs and tell everyone in the towns that they visited that Jesus was coming. When the people saw the pair of messengers coming, they knew that Jesus was soon coming. Maybe you have a friend who would like to go with you to tell others about Jesus just as the pairs did a long time ago. When you see two things that belong together like salt and pepper, you will remember that once Jesus sent out two people together to tell others about God's love.

WE ARE FREE!

John 8:31-36, vs. 32: . . . and you will know the truth, and the truth will make you free.

Object: A large bell cut out of paper with one side showing a crack, representative of the Liberty Bell. It would be good if there were enough small bells to pass around.

Good morning to all of you boys and girls who are free! That should mean all of you. To be free is not something that comes easily. I hope you know that. Every once in a while there is something that happens that really helps us to understand our freedom. I have something in my hand that I am sure all of you have seen before. What do we call something that looks like this? [*Hold up bell, but hide the crack.*] A bell. Now this is a very special bell, made in Philadelphia over 200 years ago. Does anyone know what bell I mean? This bell was made to honor the idea that the people of Philadelphia were given the right to rule themselves as a free people fifty years before. One last clue. [*Turn the bell around and show them the big crack.*] If you don't know now, I am going to tell you. This is the Liberty Bell. It is one of America's richest treasures. If you go to Philadelphia sometime you will want to see the Liberty Bell.

But now I want to tell you about another kind of freedom. This freedom is spiritual freedom. When you believe in Jesus you know the truth and that will make you free spiritually. That's right, Jesus is the Liberty Bell for us. When you don't know the truth about God you are made a slave of the Devil. But when you learn about God through Jesus you are free. Jesus is like God's Liberty Bell. When we stop and think about Jesus, we feel free because we know that he forgives us all our sins.

Yes, sir, one day the people were made free citizens of Philadelphia and no longer subjects of the British. They remembered that day by making and ringing the Liberty

Bell. That's the way it is with Jesus. One day people were slaves of all kinds of sin and rules, but today because of Jesus we are free. The next time you see a picture of the Liberty Bell I want you to remember that you are free spiritually as well as being free Americans.

ALL SAINTS DAY

Matthew 5:1-12, vs. 6: Blessed are those who hunger and thirst for righteousness, for they shall be satisfied.

Object: A menu with very enticing pictures of food.

Good morning, boys and girls. How are you on this day after the Fourth of July? Oh, it wasn't the Fourth of July. I meant to say Thanksgiving. That isn't right either. What day was it? Halloween! That's right, and what do you like most about Halloween? [*Let them tell you about Halloween.*] Did you know that today is another very special day in the Church? It's special like Christmas, Easter, Pentecost and other days like that. Today is All Saints Day and we remember all of the people who have lived and died and believed in Jesus as the Son of God. They were people like you and me, not very many of them famous, but they loved the Lord Jesus with all their hearts and minds. They really wanted to be good because they knew that Jesus loved them so much.

Let me show you what I mean. Have you ever gone into a restaurant to eat? You are not quite sure what you want, so you ask to see the menu. Now the waitress brings you the menu and you open it up and now what do you do? Everything looks so good. Even the things that you don't like well look good in the pictures. It makes you so hungry and thirsty. Just look at the hamburgers and french fries and the strawberry pie with whipped cream. Even that salad looks delicious. Oh, my, am I getting hungry! I can hardly stand it, it looks so good. How many of you wish that you were sitting down and getting ready to eat that big chocolate sundae with all the nuts and whipped cream and drinking that delicious coke? You do?

Did you know that the way you feel about eating all of those good foods is the way that God wants you to feel about doing the right things for him and for other people? That's right. He wants you to be really in a hurry to do the right thing.

Jesus even says that the people who feel that they can hardly wait to love God and other people are going to be the happiest people in this world and in God's eternal world. So the next time you go into a restaurant and ask for a menu and begin to look at the pictures and think about how hungry you are, I want you to remember that you should be just that interested in doing good things for other people and for God. When you feel like that, then you will be like all the others who have believed in Jesus and you will be remembered on All Saints Day also.

JESUS STAYS WITH US

Matthew 9:18-26, vs. 19: And Jesus rose and followed him, with his disciples.

Object: Some artificial flowers and/or artificial fruit.

Good morning, boys and girls. Isn't it funny how we become so sure of some things that are not always true? For instance, some Sunday mornings, I pass in my car people who are going in the same direction that I am going and I wonder if I have ever seen them in church before. Pretty soon I get to the church and get out of my car and the people in the other car just pass right by and go somewhere else, maybe to another church. Things are not always the way they seem to be.

Let me tell you about two other things that happened to me the other day. I came home from work and I was tired and hungry. Well, the first thing that I saw when I walked through the door was a beautiful bouquet of flowers on a table. I thought to myself that I would come back and smell them as soon as I got a snack to eat before dinner. I went to the kitchen and saw a beautiful bowl of fruit on the kitchen cupboard, picked up a beautiful apple and came back to smell the flowers. Do you know what went wrong? Some of you know. Who wants to eat the apple and who wants to smell the flowers? [*Select some volunteers.*] They certainly are beautiful, aren't they? But there seems to be something wrong. What's wrong? That's right, the flowers don't smell and the fruit cannot be eaten. Things are not always what they seem to be.

Let me tell you about something else that is not always the way we think it is about Jesus. We always talk about following Jesus, going where he is to be with him. But you know, this week I read in my Bible that Jesus followed a man whose daughter was very sick. Jesus went where the man needed him. That is good to know, because sometimes we worry about whether

94

Jesus will be where we are going. It's nice to know that
Jesus will follow us wherever we need him, and that he is
not only in the places like church and school and home
but that wherever we go he will follow us and watch over
us.

A lot of times I have been told that I must follow
Jesus, but no one ever told me that Jesus would follow
me. I know now that they meant that to follow Jesus
means that I believe in him and the things that he
teaches me, but it is also nice to know that Jesus will go
with me wherever I will go. Do you see what I mean?
Things are not always the way they seem. I don't have to
go somewhere to find Jesus; Jesus will go with me wherever I am.

THERE'S ONLY ONE RIGHT WAY

*Matthew 24:15-28, vs. 24: For false Christs and false
prophets will arise and show great signs and wonders, so
as to lead astray, if possible, even the elect.*

*Object: A maze. Draw a maze with many false paths. The
center should be marked GOD. If you wish you may
make a copy with the correct path colored in and lettered
THE CHRIST.*

Good morning, boys and girls. It is nice to be at the
beginning of some things, don't you think? I like
beginnings. I like to begin games and begin to eat and
other things like that. But you know, I have to be careful
where I begin or sometimes I end up in trouble. Do you
know what I mean? Did your mother ever tell you that
you should be careful about whom you choose as friends?
Did your teacher tell you that it is very important to
begin the right way with a school problem or you won't
get the right answer?

I have something here with me this morning that
shows you what I mean. It is called a maze, and I am sure
that you have seen these in your puzzle books many
times. There are a whole lot of paths that all look alike,
but there is only one way to reach the center. Who would
like to try to help me get to the center of my puzzle?
[*Choose a volunteer.*] It is not so easy, is it? Would
someone else like to try? [*Choose another, or as many as
time permits.*] You see, there are many false paths and
only one real way to the center of the maze. Did you
know that it is the same way with real life?

Jesus told us a long time ago that there would be a lot
of what he called "false prophets" who would try to teach
us wrong ways of living. Some would say that lying is all
right or cheating is good if it helps you get the things you
want. Some of these false prophets will teach you that it
doesn't make any difference what you believe as long as

you believe something. But Jesus teaches us differently, and his teaching is that we should believe in him and no one else. He says that there is only one right way. It is just like our maze that we worked on this morning. It only has one right way to reach the center. Would you like to see the way to the center, the right way without anything blocking the path? [*Show them the second maze, this one colored in with the name JESUS CHRIST written along the path.*]

That's the way that you want to go. To make sure that you will always be on the right path, listen to Jesus and what he has to say and you will never end up in the wrong place. Be careful in the beginning and you will have a wonderful time all day and every day of your life.

BE PREPARED

Matthew 25:1-13, vs. 3: For when the foolish took their lamps, they took no oil with them; but the wise took flasks of oil with their lamps.

Object: A pair of shoes and some shoe strings which have been broken and knotted several times; a coat without buttons.

Good morning, boys and girls. Was it easy to come to church this morning? Were you prepared for church? Did you have all your clothes laid out, plenty of toothpaste for your toothbrush, and milk for your cereal? Well, if you had all of that, somebody at your house was well prepared. Who takes care of all those things at your home? Your mother? Isn't that wonderful that your mother thinks of all those things like food, toothpaste and clean clothes? Being prepared is very important, and our mothers and fathers are very good at helping us to be prepared.

I want to show you some things that I found over at Charley Careless' house the other day. First of all, old Charley was telling me how ready he always was for anything that came along. Old Charlie likes to brag a lot, so I did not pay much attention to what Charley was talking about and decided to look around. Let's see what you think after you see what I found. First here is a piece of evidence that I think you all will recognize. [*Hold up pair of shoes so that the shoestrings are in evidence.*] What do you see that is wrong with this nice pair of shoes that belong to Charley? That's right, broken shoestrings, not once or twice but many times. When I see this I know that Charley is not very well prepared. But one thing wrong is not enough to convince Charley, so I kept looking around and, sure enough, the next thing I spotted was this coat. [*Hold up coat.*] Pretty coat, but something is wrong. That's right, he is missing his buttons. Well, Charley keeps telling me that he is going to get new shoestrings and buttons but, knowing Charley, he will be walking barefooted and freezing in the cold before he gets them fixed.

The reason for telling you this story about Charley is because of something Jesus told us a long time ago. Jesus said that being prepared is very important all the time, but is especially important when we are waiting for Jesus to come into our lives. You have to buy new shoestrings before you put them in your shoes and you need a needle and thread to sew on buttons. Jesus may come at any time, and we all must be ready. You can't wait till he comes to pray, to be kind to others and to know the other things that God teaches. Don't be like Charley Careless. Be prepared.

JESUS FULFILLS GOD'S PLANS

Matthew 21:1-9, vs. 4: This took place to fulfil what was spoken by the prophet, saying, "Tell the daughter of Zion, Behold, your king is coming to you, humble, and mounted on an ass, and on a colt, the foal of an ass."

Object: A record player and a record.

Good morning, boys and girls, and welcome to Advent. That's right, it is only four weeks until Christmas. Advent is a wonderful time of the year for all of us because we take the time to think about what it is going to be like when Jesus comes back to earth to live as God has promised. But we are not here today to talk about seasons like Advent or Christmas or fall or winter. We want to talk about Jesus. Have you ever wondered what Jesus was really like? You know that there were a lot of men and women before Jesus who were good men and listened to God and told others about God. They were all good people who made a lot of promises that God said would be kept some day. Well, when Jesus came he kept the promises that other men had made for God. Let me show you what I mean.

Here is a record player. It is a good record player. Do you see all the knobs and the place where the record fits so that it will turn around? Now if I go over and plug it in and turn it on, it will do all of the things that it is supposed to do. It even promises you that it will play music. It will, too, if it has one thing. What do we have to have before the record player will play music? A record! All of the knobs, the arm that goes up and down and the table that goes around and around do nothing unless we have a record.

The record player is like all the people who made promises for God to the people, but who could not keep them. They were not supposed to keep the promises, just make them for someone else to keep. Jesus is like the record. When we put the record on and turn the knobs like the promises that were made we have this. [*Play a little of the record.*] That's right, that is the way God planned it. He wanted Jesus to keep all the promises that were made by God through the other men. Jesus is like the record. He makes everything else do what it is supposed to do. The record fulfills the record player and Jesus fulfills the promises made by the prophets who lived before him.

God has wonderful plans. One of the plans that God has made is that one day he will have a new world in which all of the people of God will live in peace and love.

GETTING READY FOR JESUS

Luke 21:25-33, vs. 28: Now when these things begin to take place, look up and raise your heads, because your redemption is drawing near.

Object: A flag and either a recording of the "Star Spangled Banner" or the music so your organist can play it.

Isn't this a fine morning to get together? Just think, there have been forty-eight Sundays in this year and, counting this one, there are four more to go. This is the last month of the year, but did you know that it is just the beginning of the church year? The church year is different, and it always gets a head start on the new year. This is the second Sunday in Advent, the first season of every Church year. This is a season of waiting and watching. Do you know what we are waiting for at this time of the year? [*See what kind of answers you get.*] Those who said Christmas or Christ's birthday are pretty close. We are waiting for Jesus to return to earth. Won't that be some great day when Jesus returns to earth? I wonder what it will be like?

Jesus said that there would be all kinds of things happening before he came back to earth, and that when these things happen in the sky we would know that he was coming. Let's see how smart we are and see if we know what to do when we see and hear signs. [*At this point have someone begin to play the "Star Spangled Banner." Listen to it for a few moments until all of the children recognize it.*] What was that? That's right, the "Star Spangled Banner." Well, you sure didn't act like you heard it. Now, let's try it again and I am going to be watching you very carefully. [*Begin the song again.*] Stop!! What do you do when you hear the "Star Spangled Banner"? Stand at attention. Put your hand over your heart, and face the flag. And if you are in uniform you salute the flag. Very good. How many of you knew the words? Do you ever sing the words? Fine. You certainly know what to do when you hear the "Star Spangled Banner" the next time.

Jesus said that someday there are going to be signs or happenings with the sun and the moon and the stars. The oceans will roar and the nations of the earth will be confused and those who are afraid will faint and then we will see Jesus coming to us from heaven. Wow! Do you know what Jesus said then? He said when you see these things happening, you should stand up and hold your head high. That means "at attention," for when Jesus comes back it will mean the start of another world.

How many of you would stand at attention for Jesus? Won't it be great to welcome him back to earth? Since we are practicing, let me see what you will do. Is everybody seated very quietly? If you saw strange things happening in the skies, and you hear the ocean roaring loudly, and unbelievers were fainting and then Jesus came to us from heaven, what would you do? [*Have them show you.*] Wonderful! You will be ready.

WHO IS JESUS?

Matthew 11:2-10, vs. 3: And said to him [Jesus], "Are you he who is come, or shall we look for another?"

Object: A three- or five-way plug and some objects to work off it, such as a razor, a lamp, a can opener, etc.

Good morning, boys and girls. Is anyone here excited about what is going to take place in a few weeks? I can remember how excited I used to be at this time of the year when I was your age. I think God likes some of the excitement he causes at this time of the year.

We know what Jesus is like and all the wonderful things he can do. But did you know that when Jesus was living in Israel and doing a lot of different things, people used to wonder if he was really the Messiah, the one sent from God, or if there maybe was some mistake. One day some of the men who were good friends of Jesus' cousin, John the Baptist, came and asked Jesus that question. "Who are you? What do you say about yourself?" It sounds strange to us that anyone would ask about who Jesus is, but they did.

Let me show you how it might have happened with a friend of mine called Perry Plug. Now Perry is really only a piece of plastic with some holes in him. Perry doesn't look like he is really worth very much, but if you were to ask Perry who he was or what he had to say for himself, why, he could tell you for hours what he has done. Let's ask old Perry Plug what he has done. [*Pretend you are talking to Perry and listening to what he says, passing the information along to the children.*] Perry, can you tell me some of the things that you have done yesterday and today? Oh, you say that you have brought light to a dark room, you gave power to a saw to cut some wood, made a big machine in a factory turn out new motors and powered a can opener for a mother getting dinner ready. Wow, Perry, that's a lot! What can you do now, so that all the boys and girls will know that you are what you say? You want me to plug in a razor, a lamp, a radio and you will make them all work. Boy, that would show them that you are really something! [*Plug them in and show them how many things it can do.*]

That's the way it was with the people who John the Baptist sent to see Jesus. They said to him, "Tell us something so that we can report it to our leader." Jesus told them that he was not going to fill their ears with words. They should look around and see all the people who had been healed by his healing and the smiles on the faces of people with hope.

You see, Perry the Plug is like Jesus. He doesn't go around telling people what he does. He leaves that to someone else. Instead he does the work that makes people glad. Is Jesus really the one God promised? Do you believe that what God did in Jesus is enough to show us how much God loves us, or should we look for another? For me, Jesus is it. I love the Lord Jesus and I pray that I may always believe what I believe today. Jesus is power, and whenever I am connected to him, just as the razor or radio is connected to Perry, I work well. When I am not, I just *look* like a disciple without really being one at all.

JOHN THE BAPTIST

John 1:19-28, vs. 22: They said to him then, "Who are you? Let us have an answer for those who sent us. What do you say about yourself?"

Object: Small packets of restaurant salt.

Boys and girls, it is only a few more days until we have a birthday party. The best birthday party in the whole world. Do you know who is going to have a tremendous birthday party this week? That's right, Jesus was born and made it Christmas Day. Pretty important day for all of us, isn't it? Can you imagine how many people in the world are going to remember that day with a special kind of celebration? More than a billion people will remember Jesus with worship and almost everyone will know that this was the day on which Jesus of Nazareth was born.

I suppose you know that Jesus had a cousin named John the Baptist who was important to the world and to Jesus. John was a strange man by the way you and I think of people. He dressed a little differently than the other people did, and he ate some different kinds of food. But we don't remember him for how he dressed or what he had to eat. No, we remember John because of the things that he did for and said about Jesus.

It would be easier for me to tell you about John the Baptist if I used one of my very good friends, Sally Salt. Now Sally does a lot of things for a lot of people like Molly Meat, Clete Celery and Lonnie Lettuce, but by herself she is almost nothing. For instance, if you went and asked Sally Salt what she could do on her own, she would tell you that she was not made to be on her own. If you said to Sally, "What do you say about yourself?" she would tell you that she was meant to prepare the meat, the celery and the lettuce. That is Sally's job, that is what she is meant for and nothing more than that. It wouldn't make any difference if you colored her, made her into big lumps or spread her out so thin there was only one grain of her in a place -- she would still be the same kind of salt.

John the Baptist is kind of like Sally Salt. People wanted to know who John the Baptist was and what he had to say for himself. They wanted to know if he was a special prophet, or even the Christ, but John said that he had come to prepare the way for Christ and that alone was his job. Nothing more nor less could be said of him. John had come to tell others about the Messiah, Jesus, and he was going to do that before he did anything else. He knew that he could not be Jesus or anybody else, but that he could do the job that God had given him. He was meant to show people, to introduce to the people, the Son of God.

John the Baptist is important to the Christian faith because he prepared the way for Jesus. Now you can understand why John the Baptist and salt are so much alike. Both of them are necessary, but by themselves they would be nothing. Sally Salt was made for Molly Meat, and John the Baptist was made for Jesus.

THE WILL OF GOD

John 21:19b-24, vs. 22: Jesus said to him, "If it is my will that he remain until I come, what is that to you? Follow me!"

Object: A toothbrush, pencil, money.

Good morning, boys and girls. Did everyone have a tremendous Christmas Day worshipping God and giving gifts to one another? How many of you remembered that it was Jesus' birthday and that this was the real reason for having Christmas? You did? Well, that's great. I sure do like Christmas because I have noticed that people are different at Christmas time than at any other time of the year. Even things that would often make them sad at any other time do not seem to do so at this time of the year. People want to be happy. They *will themselves* to be happy, so they are happy.

How many of you know what it means *to will* something to be done? Suppose, for instance, that I told you that I got up this morning, took my toothbrush and made my teeth clean. You could say that I *willed* my teeth clean. I wanted them clean so I made them clean. It was my will that made me do it. Or suppose that I took this pencil and wrote a letter to my best friend, Homer. Then you could say that I willed myself to write a letter. I want to show you that it is important how you use your will, for it can be used in a bad sense as well as a good sense. You could will yourself to start a fight or say something mean, just as you can use this money to buy something good or something bad. Your will is important and God gave you a will to use freely just as he uses his will.

God has a will, too. Let me tell you about a time when Jesus spoke about the will of God. One day Peter and Jesus were having a discussion and they were talking about the time each of them would spend here on earth.

Jesus knew that he was returning in a very short time to his Heavenly Father. He had also told Peter that at some time he would die in a way like Jesus had died on a cross. But Peter wanted to know about the others, people like John, the disciple. Jesus said that it was his will that John should remain here on earth for a long time after the others had died. That was the will of God and that means that Jesus wanted it that way and that nothing else could change it.

Our time on earth is given to us as a special gift by the will of God, and he gives us a will to use while we are here. God uses his will always for our good. Now you know what it means when we talk about the will of God. It means that God is doing what he knows is best for his world and his people.